# You have no idea

# YOU HAVE NO IDEA

## A Famous Daughter, Her No-Nonsense Mother, and How They Survived Pageants, Hollywood, Love, Loss (and Each Other)

## VANESSA WILLIAMS
## AND HELEN WILLIAMS

### With Irene Zutell

GOTHAM BOOKS

GOTHAM BOOKS
Published by Penguin Group (USA) Inc.
375 Hudson Street, New York, New York 10014, U.S.A.
Penguin Group (Canada), 90 Eglinton Avenue East, Suite 700, Toronto, Ontario M4P 2Y3, Canada
(a division of Pearson Penguin Canada Inc.); Penguin Books Ltd, 80 Strand, London WC2R 0RL,
England; Penguin Ireland, 25 St Stephen's Green, Dublin 2, Ireland (a division of Penguin Books
Ltd); Penguin Group (Australia), 250 Camberwell Road, Camberwell, Victoria 3124, Australia
(a division of Pearson Australia Group Pty Ltd); Penguin Books India Pvt Ltd, 11 Community
Centre, Panchsheel Park, New Delhi–110 017, India; Penguin Group (NZ), 67 Apollo Drive,
Rosedale, Auckland 0632, New Zealand (a division of Pearson New Zealand Ltd); Penguin Books
(South Africa) (Pty) Ltd, 24 Sturdee Avenue, Rosebank, Johannesburg 2196, South Africa

Penguin Books Ltd, Registered Offices: 80 Strand, London WC2R 0RL, England

Published by Gotham Books, a member of Penguin Group (USA) Inc.

First printing, April 2012
1  3  5  7  9  10  8  6  4  2

Copyright © 2012 by Devsha, LLC

Unless otherwise noted, all photos are courtesy of Mellian Group Archives, Vanessa Williams
Personal Archives, and Helen Tinch Williams Family Archives.

Photo/Archive Research: Brian Edwards

Photo/Memorabilia Restoration: Scott Hoover, PG Productions, and Michael Chanslor

Front jacket wardrobe styling: Vanessa Williams—suit dress by Carmen Marc Valvo, gold-tone
necklace worn as bracelet by Jennifer Miller, hoop earrings by BenAnein. Helen Williams—
suit dress by Carmen Marc Valvo, bracelet by BenAnein.

Back jacket wardrobe styling: Vanessa Williams—gown by Carmen Marc Valvo, earrings by
Jennifer Miller. Helen Williams—gown by Marie Saint Pierre.

Gotham Books and the skyscraper logo are trademarks of Penguin Group (USA) Inc.

LIBRARY OF CONGRESS CATALOGING-IN-PUBLICATION DATA
has been applied for.

ISBN 978-1-592-40707-1

Printed in the United States of America
Set in Dante MT Std. and Avenir Roman
Designed by Susan Hood Design

To my parents, Helen and Milton Williams, whom I thank for making me grounded. Everything always returns to the incredibly strong foundation you built for me and Chris. I pray that my efforts reach half of what you both were able to give me throughout my life.

—*Vanessa Williams*

To milton, for a depth of love for me and an acceptance of who I am that had no bounds.

To vanessa and chris, for becoming adults who make positive contributions to society—that gives me parental pride.

To my "grands," who make me smile with wonderment while I try to grasp and understand their zeal for the cyber-space world.

To my sister gretta: You have no idea how much I miss you.

—*Helen Williams*

YOU HAVE NO IDEA

# THRILL RIDES

*Do not ride your bike with another kid on the back. You could kill yourself.*

—HELEN WILLIAMS

My school report cards say I was the kid who obeyed rules and followed directions. But my mother tells a much different tale. When Mom told me *not* to do something, I did it anyway. The thrill of the adventure, the adrenaline rush, and the escape trumped all consequences. And there were always consequences—because no matter how quiet, sneaky, and brilliant I thought I was, I couldn't outsmart Mom.

It was the summer of 1972 and I was heading into fourth grade with Mr. Hart (that's how I remember the early years—grade and teacher). My three cousins from Baltimore were staying at our Millwood, New York, home during their annual visit. Gabby, the youngest, was always my partner in crime. We decided to explore the neighborhood by bike.

I had just traded up from my little-girl bike with the banana seat (they had been the rage—all the *Brady Bunch* sisters had them) to a big-girl green six-speed that my dad had found in a trash heap on the side of the road and repaired. I pulled it out of the garage and jumped on. Since Gabby didn't have a bike with her, she walked next to me. I figured when we were a few houses down the street on Glenwood Road, Gabby would jump on the newspaper rack over the back tire.

Mom knew exactly what I was thinking.

"Don't ride that bike with Gabby on the back," she said. "It's too dangerous. You could kill yourself. Take turns."

I nodded, but was thinking, *I can handle this.*

A few minutes later, I hooked a left onto the quiet, crescent-shaped road. "Jump on the back," I told Gabby.

She sat sidesaddle and wrapped her arms around me. I pumped my legs and pulled at the handlebar, balancing the bike perfectly. We headed toward a hill—always the best part of my daily bike ride. I loved to coast down it, let go of the handlebar, balance, and fly.

I coasted as we gained speed downhill, laughing as the wind whipped through our hair. I tightened my grip, freewheeling so fast that everything became a dizzying blur. It was exhilarating, until . . .

The handlebar started vibrating and the bike wobbled. In a sickening flash, I realized that because there was too much weight on the back, the bike was out of control. With every muscle in my nine-year-old arms, I pulled at the handlebar to stop the wheels from weaving. But the bike couldn't handle it. The handlebar ripped off the frame.

The front tire slammed into a drainage ditch, and I sailed over the bike, still holding the handlebar.

For a second, I was flying. Then my face, hands, and knees smashed into the pavement on Glenwood Road.

You know that moment when it doesn't hurt but you know the big pain is on its way? I knew this was a big one. The gravel was embedded in my palms and knees. I slowly pushed myself up and staggered to my feet. Everything started to throb.

The handlebar had gouged out a chunk of my thigh. The pain in my mouth was unbearable, and I tasted blood. I felt around with my tongue and discovered a bloody gap in the front of my mouth. *My tooth!* I turned toward Gabby, who was on the ground, holding her knee and moaning. Once we looked at each other, we started to wail.

WAAAAH!!!!!!

Mrs. Worthy, who was the mom of the "other black family" in our small town, came running out of her house as soon as she heard us. Then she called my mom. Seconds later, it seemed, her car screeched to a stop next to us.

I wanted Mom to say, "Oh, my poor sweetheart! You must be in terrible pain. Let me hug you and everything will be fine."

Mom slammed the car door.

"What have you done to your face? Vanessa, look what you've done!"

How could she be so direct? Mom wasn't the huggy, touchy, "I love you, sweetie" type mom. She didn't show affection much, but I thought this time would somehow be different.

*Look what I've done!*

Maybe that's what this book is all about.

Eventually my face healed. My dad had to use Krazy Glue to keep in my dental cap that fell out when I ate. I spent countless hours in the dentist's chair getting root canals. (I still have a cap, but no Krazy Glue.) For months I'd cry myself to sleep because there was constant, throbbing pain from the exposed nerve where my tooth had been.

Throughout this ordeal, Mom never said, *I told you so.*

I thought Mom was being unfeeling when she stood over me while I silently begged for her affection. But in her own way, she was holding me tighter than I could really understand—she was teaching me the lesson I needed. *You did it—deal with it, learn from it. One day, the consequences will be greater and I won't be there to help you, much less carry you. Figure it out, Vanessa.*

Mom was a schoolteacher and I was her most challenging student. Throughout my life, Mom's lessons have helped me survive it all—scandal, love, marriages, divorces, disappointments, children, death, failures, success.

I'm still learning. Mom has yet to say, *I told you so.*

# Helen

The bike accident was typical Vanessa. It's the story of her life.

Vanessa always learns the hard way. Milton—her father—and I didn't have many rules, but she managed to break them. All of them. As she got older, the rules changed—but Vanessa never did. She'd do what she wanted, knowing she'd pay for it later. And she always paid for it later. (Usually with interest.) Vanessa didn't make it easy for me. She did not and she does not.

A lot of parents think it's important to be their child's friend. When Vanessa was growing up, I didn't care if she liked me. She could hate me as far as I was concerned—and sometimes I think she did. I wanted her to understand that I reacted the way I did because I knew she would continue to do things she would eventually regret. That was always my instinct with Vanessa.

When Ness was a teenager, I told her, "Never ever pose nude for anyone."

You know what happened.

Well, a little of what happened.

There's so much more.

You have no idea.

PART ONE

# INTO THE
# WOODS

*Never ever pose nude for anyone.*

—HELEN WILLIAMS

The phone call from the *New York Post* reporter seemed like just another of the hundreds of interviews I'd done since becoming Miss America ten months earlier. They were all the same—I could predict the questions: "How has your life changed?" "What's it like being the first black Miss America?" "Do you feel you've made history?" "What's next?"

I had the standard patter down: "It was an unexpected honor, with lots of pressure and great opportunity."

But "unexpected" was actually an understatement—I never had any desire to be a beauty queen, let alone Miss America. There had never been a black Miss America. Miss America was usually a blond-haired, blue-eyed girl (I do have blue eyes, though, just like my paternal grandfather, Milton Williams Sr.). I, on the other hand, was the girl who smoked pot and inhaled, drank beer at cast keg parties, and had premarital sex with my boyfriend. I lived life! Or at least I was living a twenty-one-year-old's version of life as a college junior.

My friends found the very idea of it hysterical. As we sipped our Rolling Rock beers at our theater parties before I won the crown, it became a punch line to a joke only we understood.

"Vanessa as Miss America? They have no idea who you are."

When Gary Collins, the host of the pageant, announced my name as Miss America, my first thought was, *Damn! There goes my semester abroad studying theater in London. Gotta tell Diane to get another roommate. No scones and clotted cream; no greasy fish and chips in newspaper.* My second thought was, *What am I in for? What happens after I walk down the runway of the Convention Center and head back to the fake hugs from the other contestants whose dreams had just been crushed by a pageant first-timer from New York State? Then what?*

Yikes!

And now my year was almost finished. It was Friday, July 13, 1984 (yes, Friday the 13th), and I had just six weeks left in my reign. I was in yet another hotel room on the road, the Ramada in Watertown, New York. The tiny town near the Thousand Islands, one of New York's natural wonders, was home to the New York State pageant, which I'd won last year. I was there to crown my successor.

It had been a typical day so far. Midge Stevenson, my bubbly, fit, blond chaperone and a pageant pro, had given me my itinerary in the morning. There was breakfast, pageant rehearsals, and some interviews, including this one with the *New York Post* reporter. I sat on the edge of the bed discussing Geraldine Ferraro, Walter Mondale's running mate in the upcoming presidential election and the first woman vice presidential candidate.

A first commenting on another first.

"I think it's fantastic. She'll do a wonderful job. It's a great thing for our country."

That about wrapped up the usual fifteen-minute question and answer, but before I could hang up, the reporter said, "Oh, by the way, I heard from a very reliable source that there are nude photos of you coming out in September's *Penthouse*. Is it true?"

"Excuse me?"

My heart froze. Nude pictures? Impossible.

"I don't know what you're talking about. What reliable source?"

"Well, we heard it from a very reliable source—but if you don't know about it, then I won't print it."

I hung up the phone and could not breathe.

This has got to be a mistake. Reporters always get facts wrong, right?

Plus I never signed a release for *those* pictures.

But that thought didn't calm me—instead my heart felt like it was about to explode. Is this really happening? How could I be so stupid to even get into this kind of situation?

I had to do something. My parents were on their way and I'd have to let them in on my monstrous secret. How disappointed they would be! That's the worst. The "D" word coming from the lips of your parents.

I decided to call Dennis Dowdell, a neighbor from Millwood and a corporate lawyer at American Can Company. He'd become my counsel, handling the offers that were rolling in.

I told Dennis about the reporter's question. I then confessed to the stupid summer of my nineteenth year.

"You've got to find out if this is real," I told him. He said he would. We were in detective mode, hoping to uncover a hoax.

Two years earlier, 1982, had been my "summer of freedom." I was nineteen and on a "break" from my boyfriend, Bruce Hanson, after nearly three years together. We had one of those relationships where we were almost consumed with each other. We were crazy in love. If we were apart for even a few hours it was tragic. I'd skip class or jog to meet him in the park, jumping into his waiting burgundy Camaro to make out. Once, we drove to his dorm room at Fairleigh Dickinson University, a college in Madison, New Jersey. When we were together, there was no one else in the world (except for the time my mother walked in on us in the den, stereo blasting, mid-stroke).

But what had once been so intensely pleasurable was sometimes suffocating. I told him I needed some time apart, some space. I needed to break free. I don't even think my parents knew we weren't together. They weren't fans of our relationship—and that's putting it mildly. More than once they forbade us from seeing each other. Bruce and I were a volatile combination. Too possessive, too reckless, too much for my folks to handle. Where I'd go, he'd follow. (He even transferred to Syracuse University to be with me during my freshman year.)

Bruce was handsome, with sandy brown hair and deep-set, brown, Richard Gere–like eyes—and he was white. While my mom had plenty of white friends, the idea of a white boyfriend was uncomfortable to her. She once called me into her bedroom during an episode of *The Phil Donahue Show* that was addressing the struggles interracial couples faced.

"You need to watch this," she said.

But even though this was my self-proclaimed summer of freedom, I still had to work. Every summer since I was eleven, I had some kind of job—babysitting, selling vegetables from our garden, peddling Avon cosmetics. I worked at a furrier, at a men's clothing store, a junior boutique, and a discount outlet shop.

My parents paid for my college tuition, and each year I had gotten partial scholarships for my acting, dancing, and singing. But I needed money to live on, to buy gas and spend on discount fashion. My parents wanted my younger brother, Chris, and me to learn how to be independent in case anything ever happened to them. By age three, we had learned to tie our shoes. By ten, we did our own laundry. If we had no clean clothes, that was our problem.

So I checked out the trusty PennySaver Classifieds. I found an ad for MODELS WANTED. I asked my dad what he thought and he told me to see what it was about.

A few days later, I climbed to the top floor of an old walk-up above an unpainted furniture store in Mount Kisco, New York. The sign on the door read THE MODELING REGISTRY BY TOM CHIAPEL. I walked in and was greeted by the owner—a Henry VIII lookalike, complete with a scruffy beard, jowls, and obesity.

"So you want to be a model?" Tom asked.

"Yes," I said. That would have been the easiest of all summer jobs in the world!

Then he hit me with a reality check. "I also need a receptionist plus someone who can do makeup for the models when I shoot their portfolios."

As I quickly learned, it wasn't a modeling agency—it was a "registry." All these poor hopefuls (guys included) would come for a consultation, have a lengthy discussion about their potential, and then Tom would declare: "You've got a great look. But you need a portfolio. I'll shoot it."

That was his hook: Here's the package; I'll shoot it for a good price.

And that's how he made his living. Tom also considered himself an artist. Little did I know, he would become the biggest scam artist of my life.

On shoot days, these poor suckers (myself included) would bring their own wardrobes. I'd do a full makeup job—I was hired as a makeup artist—complete with fashion contouring for black-and-white film. I'd apply blush, eyeliner, the whole nine yards, which was a lot more fun than serving fries at Burger King. Tom also snapped some "fashion shots" of me on location in a wooded area when I started working for him.

One hot summer day, Tom asked if I could stay after hours to do a shoot.

"My friend Ami is coming over. I'm going to shoot her and I'd like to use you in a few black-and-white nude silhouettes. It's going to be very artsy—you won't even see your face, only shapes and forms."

I immediately heard my mom: *Bad idea! If anyone ever asks you to pose nude, you say no!*

I knew why Mom said, "Don't take nude pictures." Mom believed I had a future that could be bright, and those pictures could one day haunt me. She also told me, "Men can be dogs." She was trying to protect me. She knew men would prey on me, and she knew how trusting I was: "You're just like your father. You'll give everyone the benefit of the doubt."

At the time I thought, *Here goes Mom again, telling me what I shouldn't do. I'm an adult now. I finished one year of college, for God's sake.*

Tom's pitch was that nudes were a work of art. I agreed. I still believe that the human body is beautiful.

There was something so freeing about doing what you're not supposed to. At nine, it was riding my bike with my cousin on the back. Ten years later, it was posing nude with a stranger.

"These are just for me. Don't worry—no one will know it's you anyway," Tom said.

Tom was my employer but also had become a friend. I'd met his wife and kids. He paid me on time and was respectful. Why shouldn't I trust him?

"Okay," I said.

Ami arrived for the photo shoot after the office closed for the day. She was about my age, maybe a little older. It was a hot summer evening in July and we drank plenty of white wine to take the edge off. Tom locked the door so we wouldn't have to worry about intruders. I was nervous and it felt like an awkward blind date. Tom probably sensed my discomfort. He knew I was a trained dancer, so he asked me to do some jumps while he photographed me.

Tom photographed solos of Ami. After he felt we had loosened up, he asked us to pose together. He positioned us and told us what to do. It felt silly, stupid, and not very artistic.

We'd pose, frozen in these awkward positions, and then wait for the next command, giggling the entire time. We were two young women giving the man behind the lens all the power in the room.

Why? Why didn't I stop it?

Part of me felt like we were being crazy and adventurous. It felt awkward having a naked woman's body so close to me, but I pretended it was no big deal. I was grown-up, artsy Vanessa. After all, this was what I wanted that summer—to break free.

A few days after the shoot, Tom showed me the contact sheets. The pictures were so tiny on the glossy paper that I had to look through a loupe to see any detail. I saw myself jumping in midair. I looked at the silhouette shots. Tom was right. You couldn't tell who those bodies belonged to on the sheet. But they were way more erotic than I remembered or had meant them to be.

It didn't matter—they were just a few rolls of film taken on a summer night on the top floor of an old building in Mount Kisco. Photos that no one would ever see.

Later that summer, I took a Metro-North train from Chappaqua to Grand Central Terminal. As I was making my way through the maze of commuters, a meek-looking man with wire-rimmed glasses approached me.

"Excuse me, I'm a photographer. Do you model?"

*Not another one*, I thought. Here we go again.

But when Gregg Whitman pulled out his portfolio, his photography was not only edgy and strong but also feminine and romantic. He seemed to be a better photographer than Tom Chiapel.

"You've got a great exotic look that Europeans love," he said, explaining that he did a lot of work for the foreign market. "I would love to do some testing with you."

I took his information, thought about it, and gave him a call.

A few days later, Bruce (yes, we were back together) drove me to the photo shoot on Steinway Street in Astoria, Queens. I wasn't familiar with this neck of the woods, even though I considered myself a seasoned New Yorker. Of course, Gregg's "studio" was also his apartment.

(Ding! Ding! Ding! Escape, escape! But guess who stayed? And this time I couldn't use booze as an excuse.)

Bruce was concerned and asked if I wanted him to come with me, but I assured him that I'd be fine and told him to pick me up later.

We started the shoot on a nearby street. I'd brought my wardrobe—a floral, black chiffon dress; Union Jack jogging shorts; boots; and scarves. Gregg took some typical New York City shots—I posed on top of a cab and on a front stoop. Then we headed back to his place.

That's when he asked me to take a chance and go for more revealing setups. They'd be beautiful, provocative, and alluring, he said.

A classmate, Shelby, had given me a gorgeous burgundy scarf for my eighteenth birthday from Abels, the ritzy store in Mount Kisco, and I'd brought it along for the shoot. I undressed and wrapped my nineteen-year-old cellulite-free bottom in it. I turned my back to the camera, pretending to be a vixen instead of a teenager using a graduation gift as a prop in an adult-only photo.

Then Gregg showed me some S-and-M, Helmut Newton–style photos. The images were strong, but the lighting seemed to soften the kinky message a bit.

"Can we try for something like this?" he asked. "Trust me. It will be beautiful."

He took out a leather contraption that looked part G-string, part nippleless bikini bra top, complete with a studded collar around the neck. I held it in my hands and studied it. It was so not me. But I thought, *Okay, let me be daring and adventurous.* I went in the bathroom and put it on.

*What am I doing? I started out on top of a cab and ended up in a dog collar! Have I lost my mind?*

*Mom, this is when I need you to rescue me!*

As adventurous and strong as I've always been, there was also a part of me that failed to speak up when I needed to. I don't know why this is—it's just how I've always been for as long as I can remember.

But I headed into Gregg's room, pretending that being dressed like this was no big deal. Gregg told me how to stand and he began to snap away.

The poses Gregg positioned me in didn't feel artsy to me; they felt dirty—no matter how good the lighting was. I knew I shouldn't be doing them. I'd never even seen an outfit like this.

I felt all the energy just drain from my body.

After shooting barely a roll of film in the bondage getup, Gregg asked me what was wrong. I told him I didn't want to do this anymore. I got dressed and couldn't wait to escape Queens.

Bruce was waiting out front in his car and I jumped in. We sped back to the safety of my home. I didn't say a word about the shoot, but it was eating away at me. I tried to act as normal as possible, and Bruce bought my act.

A few days later I told Bruce about my bonehead decisions and that we had to go get those negatives.

But when we got to Gregg's apartment, he wouldn't give them back. He said they were "our child" and he didn't want to "give up our child."

(This is where the creepy music plays.)

But Bruce and I were a team and we wouldn't leave. After a few minutes of pestering, Gregg went back and returned with a pile of negatives.

Whew! Problem solved—or so I thought.

Thinking back on that ordeal as I sat in the hotel after my phone interview, it dawned on me that Gregg must have kept some of the photos and sold them to *Penthouse*. It couldn't have been Tom—he was a friend!

I sat waiting for Dennis to call. How was I ever going to break the news to my parents? It had been an extraordinary year for them. They'd been so proud.

I prayed for guidance. I prayed that this was all a big mistake.

The phone finally rang. My heart pounded in my ears. It was Dennis.

"Sorry to tell you this, but it's true. The September issue of *Penthouse* has you on the cover and photos of you with another woman."

What? Tom? Impossible! I never signed a release. He promised me no one would ever see them.

Shit!

We had just walked into Vanessa's hotel room, excited to see our daughter who had been away for so long. It was supposed to be a happy occasion in one of the best years of our lives. I wish every parent could experience the joy we experienced watching our daughter crowned Miss America. Parts of it were so exhilarating, so rewarding, so fun.

But when Vanessa opened the door she didn't look happy to see us. She looked petrified. She couldn't speak. Vanessa at a loss for words? It was my turn to be petrified. This was going to be really, really bad.

Vanessa choked back sobs and blurted it out. "There are these nude photos of me coming out in *Penthouse*. I have no idea what they're going to look like. I'm sorry. I'm so, so sorry."

She couldn't stop apologizing. She couldn't stop sobbing. I knew that telling us was the hardest thing she'd ever done.

Wait a minute. Nude pictures? When? How? Who? And *why*?

Her father and I were stunned. I was too stunned to speak—and that was a good thing because I don't know what I would have said—or yelled.

Raising Vanessa had always been a challenge. I thought I was always ready for anything. But nudity? I wasn't prepared for this.

Her father walked over to her and hugged her tight. I joined him, and the three of us just held on to one another for a long, long time. I knew the next few months were going to be tough. I knew the press would be merciless. I knew Vanessa needed us, even though part of me wanted to scream, "WHAT WERE YOU THINKING?"

"It's all right," we said. "We're always on your side. We love you and we're always here for you."

You could see this pressure being lifted off her after she told us. As tough as the next few months would be, the hardest part for Vanessa was telling us. Now that she had done that and had our support, she felt that she could handle the onslaught.

When the photos came out, I asked Milton, "Aren't you going to look at them?" He shook his head. He could not speak about it. It was all too much for him. But me? Of course I had to see for myself what Vanessa had done. Milton knew I'd look, but he never asked me about them and I never brought it up. I closed the door to my bedroom, took a deep breath, and prepared myself for anything. I didn't know how I'd feel—if I'd be furious or just plain sick.

When I saw the pictures I wasn't angry, just very sad. I stared at them and tried to get into Vanessa's head. I knew exactly what had happened. I understood how the photographer had been able to cajole her. He fed into Vanessa's need to be daring.

While the world focused on her naked body, I looked into her eyes. They looked so confused, so sad. The look said to me, "Oh my God, what am I doing here?" As daring as Vanessa wanted to believe she was, she wasn't really daring at all. I could see she was so uncomfortable, so out of place.

I could also see that she was thinking of me. She was hearing my voice telling her not to do the very thing she was doing.

*I started out posing on top of a city cab and ended up inside with a studded collar around my neck.*

# CHAPTER 2

*If you are going to do something questionable, ask yourself, "Is this something that would make my parents proud?" If the answer is no, don't do it.*

—HELEN WILLIAMS

Vanessa, naked photos? What were you thinking?"

I still get asked that question to this day! People will say, "You're an intelligent woman; how could you think nude pictures wouldn't come out if you became famous? Especially if you became Miss America?"

Well, guess what? I never imagined I'd be any type of beauty queen, that's for sure—let alone Miss America! Even when I'd sprawl at the foot of my parents' bed and watch the Miss America pageant with Mom, I didn't stare at the brightly lit runway thinking one day I would be on that very stage. Instead, we critiqued the gowns, cracked on the stiff hair, laughed at some of the "unique" talents, and rooted for a winner. Miss America was an American tradition, the granddaddy of the pageant world.

And it was rare to see anyone who looked like me.

Growing up in Millwood, I never ever thought of myself as beautiful. My mother emphasized early on to focus on accomplishment rather than appearance. Even the women I considered gorgeous—Lena Horne, Diahann Carroll, Jayne Kennedy—had talents that transcended their looks. My mother would watch other women like them and say to me, "Talented, bright, rather pretty." I realize now that she was subtly explaining to me that looks can only get you so far. When I graduated from Horace Greeley High School in Chappaqua, I wasn't voted prom queen or Best Looking. I was voted Best Actress. And that meant the world to me.

Back in my day, preppy was the style, and the "beautiful" girls in school didn't resemble me at all. They were wraithlike with straight blond hair. They wore Fair Isle sweaters and Izod shirts. They skied on winter break, played tennis at the clubs in the summer, and had names like Leigh, Paige, and Blythe. I was different because my hair wasn't straight and blond and my butt was "athletic." I even got asked once, "Do you have an afro down there?" Sometimes my mom would say, "Stop poking out your lips," when I wasn't even doing anything! I have full lips that I thank God for—especially now that most white women want them. Crazy how times have changed.

Being the only black kid in class, I knew I was different. When the kids would do their classroom matchmaking in grade school, they would always suggest I "go out" with Jacob, the Indian kid, because he was the other brown kid in the grade.

When those adolescent hormones invaded my body, I got pimples. I'd dot my face with Rezamid before I went to bed and pray the bumps would disappear by morning. I also had a cap over my chipped front tooth that didn't quite match the rest of my grill—but it never stopped me from smiling.

My fellow Miss America contestants had been doing the pageant circuit since they were little girls. They dreamed of becoming Miss

America. I was not a seasoned pro who competed in the Little Miss America pageant at the Palisades Amusement Park on the other side of the Hudson River. But the other contestants *were* pageant pros and could recite one another's statistics. They knew the correct poses when they strolled along the stage in their evening gowns. They knew the proper way to walk in their swimsuits down the runway, pause, and then turn. It was all very studied. It was all very processed. It was all very not me.

People will still come up to me and say, "Tell me your tricks from your pageant days."

What tricks? I didn't learn any secrets. There was no Vaseline on my upper teeth. I wasn't taught a special walk or wave. I didn't smear Preparation H under my eyes. I wasn't one of those girls. Even as I would glide down the runway in high heels and a swimsuit, I would think: *How did I get here? Now, how do I justify this again? Oh yeah, scholarship money for my junior year! You're an actress. Pretend this is another role. And smile!*

How did Miss America happen? I don't know the behind-the-scenes machinations. So I asked George Miserlis, an actor, friend, and former Syracuse classmate to fill me in on the details. All I remember is that during my sophomore year as a musical theater major at Syracuse University, I was being watched. One night, I sang "The Second Time Around" during a school production of *Swingin' on a Star!*, a revue of the works of composer Jimmy Van Heusen (who actually came to watch the show). And this is what happened—according to George:

George's friend Bill Harmand was on the board of Miss Greater Syracuse, a preliminary round of Miss America. He wanted to see the fall review at Syracuse because the cast members are considered some of the most talented students at the university. (Aaron Sorkin, the Emmy- and Academy Award–winning screenwriter, was also cast in this small musical.)

After the show, George went up to Bill, who looked as if he were holding in a big secret, his eyes bulging out of his head.

"You look weird," George said. "Did you like the show or not?"

Bill shrugged his shoulders. "How well do you know this Vanessa?"

"What do you mean, 'this Vanessa'?"

Bill told George that he thought I had what it took to go all the way to Miss America. He wanted to present me to the board of directors at an informal party.

George told me about what Bill had said, but I didn't answer right away. "Let me think about it," I said.

The next day after jazz class, I went up to George and asked for Bill's number. I still wasn't convinced that this was something I wanted to pursue. Me—a beauty queen? I don't think so!

But Vicki Longley, the director of the Miss Greater Syracuse pageant, came to visit me, and she was persistent. Vicki was a blond, exuberant woman in her thirties. She knew everything there was to know about pageants. It was her calling, her passion. She'd done the circuit herself, and was also an entrepreneur. She owned a catering company and knew a lot about fine cuisine. She lived in a Tudor home with wall-to-wall ivory carpeting. She was like the Martha Stewart of Syracuse.

Last year, Vicki had scouted the Syracuse opera singer who had won Miss Greater Syracuse and went on to compete in Miss New York.

This year I was her obsession.

I was not a pageant girl. I was an actor, just cast as the Orange Girl in *Cyrano de Bergerac* at Syracuse Stage, a repertory company on campus. The part was not a lead, but would award me some points toward an Actors' Equity card, which is the track to being a professional on the Broadway stage. One more step closer to the path of Meryl.

I loved Meryl Streep. My first acting teacher, Phil Stewart, turned me on to her. I watched all her movies, studied her dialects, and marveled at her expressions. Her accents were impeccable and she was ethereal. I wanted to follow in her footsteps. So that was the plan—major in musical theater at Syracuse, junior year abroad in London, graduate from Syracuse with a BFA, head to Yale for postgraduate theater studies, and then on to Broadway.

But *Cyrano* was canceled, and now I was free in April. It was time to think about scholarship money for junior year.

Vicki *did* mention scholarship money.

If I won Miss Greater Syracuse, I'd earn five hundred dollars for school next year. I mentioned this to my mom, who was always applying for scholarships in dance, singing, and acting for me. Over the years I'd received money from various places—the National Foundation for Advancement in the Arts, the Westchester County Chapter of Links, and Elejmal Temple.

Without missing a beat, Mom said, "Do it."

Miss Greater Syracuse is the local step to Miss America, with the same competitions—talent, swimsuit, and evening gown. I figured talent would be a cinch—just sing a song from performance class. I had to do that weekly—no big deal. "The Music and the Mirror" from *A Chorus Line* was a number that I could sing and dance to, so I would be able to showcase my talents. But then I thought, *Ehhh . . . too much effort.*

"Being Good Isn't Good Enough" was a song I'd been assigned in performance class. Leslie Uggams sang it in the Broadway musical *Hallelujah, Baby!* The song contained the lyrics, "I'll be the best or nothing at all." It had a strong, beautiful melody and I knew that no one had done it in the competition before. I'd just belt it out and "lift that cloud." (That's what Brent Wagner, the head of the musical theater department, would have us imagine when we raised our arms during the end of the number.)

I bought an aqua-blue one-piece bathing suit with black piping at Sibley's, a downtown Syracuse department store. Then a group of us headed to the auditorium for Miss Greater Syracuse. I told my parents not to bother making the long drive up because it was not a big deal. Tim Thayer, my friend and mentor, accompanied me on the piano. I had my core group of friends in the audience, ready for a good laugh and, of course, ready to be rowdy and cheer me on.

And then, lo and behold, I actually won the damn thing!

We celebrated with cold Rolling Rocks back at the railroad apartment Bruce and I shared. I spent more time there than my Grover Cleveland dorm room. We passed my silver tray around so everyone could read the inscription: VANESSA WILLIAMS, MISS GREATER SYRACUSE, 1983.

I called my parents.

"Guess what . . . I won!" I told my mom.

"That's terrific! How much money did you get?"

Vicki went into production mode to prepare me for the state's Miss New York pageant. "Now let's practice interviews," Vicki would say. Then she'd turn on a tape recorder as she asked me questions. "Did you hear how many times you said, 'um,' or 'you know'?"

She even made me sing into a wooden spoon in her living room. Wow! For anyone who's a seasoned pro on stage, the wooden spoon gag is pretty humiliating. But I sucked it up and did it for Vicki.

Vicki once took me to a fine French restaurant—I'm sure to check out my table manners, which my parents had taught me well. She introduced me to local designer Eugene Taddeo, who added more clothes to my wardrobe for the trip to the "States."

Then it was off to Miss New York. You'd probably assume the pageant would take place in Manhattan, but you'd be wrong. It's held in Watertown, New York. Way up at the top of New York State, bordering Canada by the Thousand Islands. (That's where Thousand Island salad dressing originated.) And that's where I headed in July for the next leg of my beauty pageant circuit, armed with my Miss Greater Syracuse sash and my crown in its wooden box.

And what do you know—I won that, too!

I was happy about it. *Money!* A few thousand for my semester abroad! But here we go again: What's my role? What are my duties?

When I won Miss New York, I had no idea what that meant and what it entailed. Soon I found myself at parades in the farm belt. I'd sit in a car, waving at tractors and cows. I was thinking, *Shouldn't I be in a show right now? I always do theater in the summer.* But I saw this as a temporary interruption from doing what I loved. This was just a little detour and then I'd be back on track to Broadway.

Now don't get me wrong—I'm no city slicker. I grew up in a small town and I loved rural living. We had family friends who owned a farm where we'd visit, drive tractors, collect eggs, the whole works. But me waving at tractors? It was an out-of-body experience. I considered it my job for the summer. The year before, I'd worked at a model registry; this year, I was waving in small-town parades.

Besides appearing at parades, luncheons, and county fairs, I had to pick out material for the dresses I'd wear in the Miss America pageant. Vicki was still in charge and went over every aspect of the pageant circuit—the competitions, the way to walk, the way to turn at the end of the runway and look at the judges. She prepped me on questions I'd probably be asked during the interview session with the judges.

Even though I'd won the talent portion at Miss New York with "Being Good Isn't Good Enough," Vicki suggested a different song—Barbra Streisand's arrangement of "Happy Days Are Here Again."

"People aren't familiar with your song, but everyone knows 'Happy Days Are Here Again.' It's important to pick a song the judges have heard before," she explained. I listened to it and knew I could nail it.

Vicki would conduct more mock interviews at her kitchen table. "What's your favorite book? Movie? TV show?" She'd tape it, then hit rewind and play it back for me. I still said "um" and "you know" too much, she told me.

She would add her two cents, guide me through what she'd do or say, but I never was given any of that processed patter that so many beauty contestants have. I did ask for her help on one question that I had no idea how to answer: "Why is it necessary to have a swimsuit competition?"

She told me to say something like, "A fit body reflects a fit mind."

I loved the perks that came with winning—one of which was free clothes. You would think Miss New York would go to Madison Avenue and pick out Halston gowns (I ended up getting an original Halston gown when I met the designer at my first state dinner at the White House as Miss America). Instead I headed to Ursula of Switzerland in Schenectady, New York, where the gowns and dresses were dipped in sequins and chiffon and had puffy sleeves and asymmetrical hemlines. Not my personal style but fit for a queen.

My mom, Vicki, and I would also shop at fabric stores in New York City's garment district. Vicki chose the colors I should wear and told me what to avoid. "You can't wear reds or purples—those are too ethnic," she said.

I did wear a red sheath gown for the parade on the Boardwalk and in the Miss America portrait. But we settled mostly on light tones: a pale lavender gown and a nude-colored sparkly gown, as well as an aqua-sequined gown—to make my eyes pop—with two enormous rosettes on the shoulders. Vicki picked everything. She'd sketch her designs on paper and then start on the original creations. Even the outfits she didn't design, she bedazzled. We picked out my evening gown at Sibley's, the department store from which I had purchased my bathing suit for Miss Greater Syracuse. It was an ivory Grecian dress. Very understated. Vicki studded it with crystals. She loved accoutrements. I think she thought that everything looked better when it sparkled.

Escorted by my chaperone, Lynn Caterson, I was the first contestant to arrive in Atlantic City, which got me unintended press. It was Sunday, September 11, and all was abuzz for the fifty-ninth Miss America pageant.

There was a lot of nervous energy in the Convention Center, as it began to fill up with girls who were "homegrown for pageants," as my mom put it. There were girls who had starved themselves, girls who had practiced the same routines since they were children, girls who'd been coached by their moms since birth, and girls who'd been in hundreds of pageants. There were only a handful of us first-timers. We found one another, stuck together, and bonded over our rookie status. We were naive and ready to have fun.

On Saturday, the night of the televised pageant, we opened with a song, "Go for It All." I had on a white knitted two-piece top and skirt with leg-of-mutton sleeves. Vicki had dotted the entire ensemble with Swarovski crystals.

I guess Vicki had missed the memo that there were to be no sparkles for the opening number. Well, Wanda Gayle Geddie, Miss Mississippi, who'd been in the pageant circuit forever, gave me the news: "You can't wear that. Don't you know? Sparkles in the opening number are forbidden."

*I didn't know.*

So Vicki quickly devised a solution. She pushed the crystals through the fabric so they couldn't be seen. Problem solved. Competition noted.

Wanda thought she could rattle me, but her plan didn't work. She wound up in fourth place.

Until I arrived for the pageant, I'd never been to Atlantic City. I knew about the Boardwalk and saltwater taffy from watching the pageant as a kid. On television, the pageant seemed so spectacular, but the reality was very different. It was a mom-and-pop operation run primarily by volunteers who were mostly Atlantic City house-wives and business folk. It was not a big, well-oiled machine like most people assumed.

The Atlantic City Convention Center, where the pageant took place, was a neo-Romanesque building constructed in 1929. It was a big old barn of a place with an enormous arched roof, 137 feet high. I don't remember it feeling glitzy or glamorous. It had worn carpets, huge chandeliers, burgundy and gold drapes, booming acoustics, and that Boardwalk scent—a mix of seawater, mold, and mildew.

Miss America didn't have a huge staff. All fifty contestants did their own hair and makeup in a big room filled with folding tables and mirrors. I brought my heated roller set, a big can of hair spray, and my palette of Fashion Fair cosmetics (the only makeup made exclusively for black women at the time). My chaperone helped me through the chaos to get ready for the live telecast. She grabbed me, attacked my head with spray, and then scrunched my hair with her fingers. Who was this person with the perky hairdo staring back at me in the mirror? I'd never scrunched my hair that tight, but I couldn't do anything about it.

Before we got to Saturday night's live telecast, we went through the other preliminary rounds to determine the top ten contestants. The first night of the competition was on Wednesday. I won swim-suit. Cool. Thursday was evening gowns. It wasn't a competition, so no pressure. Friday was talent. I sang "Happy Days Are Here Again." It felt great. I hit all the notes. Nailed it. Wowed the crowd. The judges liked it, too—because I won. The odds were if you win both swimsuit and talent competitions, you win the crown. But still, I had my doubts. I thought, *Okay, at least I'll make it into the top ten.* And I did.

The final televised pageant was a dizzying blur—I barely knew what was going on around me. It was night number four and millions were watching at home. My nightly cheering section from New York, who always made me feel great each time I stepped onto the stage, was there in full force.

My name was called in the top ten on stage. As Miss New York, I was ready to do it all again live. I walked onto the stage in my ivory gown and introduced myself to the audience. I said that my goal was to one day have a successful career on Broadway. Later, I belted out "Happy Days Are Here Again" and strode onstage in my white one-piece. I felt great and confident. There was no pressure. I'd won these competitions already, so this was for the camera—and it was fun.

Suzette Charles, Miss New Jersey, also sang a Barbra Streisand song, "Kiss Me in the Rain." She had an extraordinary voice and she was also of color (her father was Italian and her mother was black). Even though I'd won swimsuit and talent, Suzette was a pageant pro and this was her hometown. She had been Little Miss New Jersey in the Little Miss America pageant; she sang in the Atlantic City casinos and had been on shows like *Sesame Street* and *The Electric Company* as a little girl; she was the hometown sweetheart. I knew that if she won, I'd be runner-up. I'd hug her, congratulate her, and then head off to London. That was the plan.

Gary Collins, the pageant host, announced the runners-up—fourth, third, second—and my name wasn't called. Then . . . first runner-up: Suzette Charles.

This could only mean one thing.

"Six of the brightest and loveliest young women in America are standing on our stage," Gary said. "One of them will be the new

Miss America and the winner of a twenty-five thousand dollar scholarship. And our new Miss America is . . . Vanessa Williams!"

As Debra Maffett, the 1983 Miss America, put the rhinestone crown on my head, I thought, *There goes my junior year abroad in London.* The applause thundered and ricocheted off the tin roof as I walked along the runway, smiling, waving, and thinking. Some said I strutted down the runway. *What happens next?* I had no idea. I had no idea that I'd be traveling twenty thousand miles a month, changing locations every twenty-four to forty-eight hours. I had no idea that in a few weeks I'd be dining with the president and first lady. I didn't know anything yet. I just knew I wouldn't be taking a plane to England.

It was a strange feeling to be the center of such a big event but to feel so detached. I had no emotion—I wasn't happy. I wasn't excited. I wasn't there.

I just smiled and waved, smiled and waved.

I went to the end of the runway and turned. Then I made my way along the platform toward the New York delegation. It was the last stop of my winner's walk.

The clapping and hooting and hollering were louder and more intense there than anywhere else in the room. There was a whole bunch of my family—my mom, dad, and brother; my aunts and uncles; and my grandmother, plus a lot of other relatives and friends. A big group had rented a bus and taken it from Buffalo. They were all standing up and clapping like this was the greatest moment of their lives. They were going crazy. I swear, through the din I could hear my dad—who always clapped the loudest and the longest. The excitement brought me out of my trance and snapped me back into my body. That's when it hit me: *Wow, this is a big deal. A huge deal.*

Up until that moment I was just going through the motions. I hadn't thought about what it meant.

I was Miss America. The first black Miss America.

I'd made history.

It was thrilling. It was unbelievable. It was crazy.

It was also scary . . . but I didn't know that yet.

⁓

On the front of Vanessa's birth announcement there's a drawing of a smiling baby girl wearing a big crown and holding a scepter.

It reads, "Here she is—Miss America. She's also known as Vanessa Lynne."

I had searched the aisles of the local Hallmark store until I found the perfect card. I bought it because it was cute and funny. I never in my wildest dreams imagined it would also be true.

When we arrived in Atlantic City for the pageant, it was like entering a different world—a world we didn't know existed. These were all serious pageant people. Even the parents were dressed with glitz and glamour. All they talked about was pageants, pageants, pageants. These parents looked at Milton and me in our plain clothes without even a speck of adornment and, well, they thought we were so not of their element. We got a big laugh out of it.

There was a parents' luncheon and all anyone could talk about was how many crowns their daughters had won, how many pageants they'd been in. They asked us about Vanessa's pageant history. I shrugged and said, "She has no pageant experience." Most were shocked to hear this. I enjoyed telling them because I loved to watch them get ticked off and see their expressions of disbelief and surprise.

We were on another planet—a very glittery planet—thanks to Vanessa.

There was no question in my mind that Vanessa was the most poised. I wasn't surprised when she won the swimsuit competition—

she was always in good shape. And she really looked so stunning in her evening gown with her hair up. She made a great impression on the audience. Some of these girls seemed so programmed, but Ness was a natural and so unpretentious.

And talent? Well, of course Vanessa has talent. She gets it all from me!

They started calling the names of the runners-up. When it got to the last two, I figured Vanessa might be possibly the first runner-up. Suzette Charles, Miss New Jersey, would be the winner. She'd grown up on pageants and this was her dream. She was also black, so I thought if they're going to have a black Miss America, it would be someone who was pageant oriented.

But then Suzette Charles's name was announced as first runner-up.

I nudged Milton. "I don't believe it! Vanessa pulled it off. She really did it."

When Vanessa was named Miss America, the place went wild. There were a lot of people pulling for her. Our friends just erupted into cheers and applause. We were all on our feet, screaming. It was such an indescribable moment to see your child win Miss America, to make history. I was so proud of her.

And her father? He was always the first to clap, the last to stop, and the loudest.

During the first few days, the mail was incredible. We got thousands of notes congratulating Vanessa. But a week after Vanessa won, reality set in. The tone of some of the letters changed. Someone wrote that they were going to throw acid in her face. People sent notes: "YOU'RE DEAD, BITCH," "You'll Never Be Our Miss America," "You're all black scum."

I gasped the first time I saw some of the contents. Some letters had pubic hair in them; some had spit; some had semen. I went to the police. They had an agent from the FBI show me how to open mail, so, if necessary, they could take some of the letters and trace them back to where they originated. I wore gloves and opened the mail with a letter opener. I'd never take the stuff out—it was just too disgusting. I gave some to the police and kept the others.

We experienced racism from both camps—black and white. We got letters from black people saying we were liars—that she wasn't really black. How could she be black with light skin and blue eyes? We'd go to hell for our deceptions. Then we got letters from white people saying that she shouldn't be Miss America because she's mixed blood. She's not pure. She's not Miss America material.

We were so worried about Vanessa when she was on the road, but we didn't tell her everything because we didn't want her to be afraid. At certain appearances, they'd have extra security. Milton and I were especially nervous when she'd be in towns in the South where there were still members of the Ku Klux Klan. They had to put armed guards outside her hotel room in Alabama. They wouldn't let her ride in convertibles there. There were sharpshooters on the roofs of buildings during her hometown parade through Millwood and Chappaqua. Her car was flanked by police officers.

When Vanessa won, we had been excited for her year-long reign as Miss America. We had no idea that there'd be all this anger and hatred. We had no idea that her Miss America reign would quickly become a reign of terror for us. We had no idea how once it started, we couldn't wait for it to be over.

And we had no idea that Ness had a past that could come back and haunt her.

**1 and 2:** The newly crowned Miss New York, July 16, 1983. **3:** Meeting Muhammad Ali during pageant week. **4:** With my wonderful chaperones Midge Stevenson and Ellie Ross. **5:** Signing my first autographs as Miss America. **6:** The evening gown competition. **7:** With Los Angeles mayor Tom Bradley in 1984, being honored at the NAACP seventy-fifth anniversary event. **8:** After winning both the Preliminary Swimsuit and Talent Awards. I became one of only thirteen Miss Americas to accomplish this feat in the pageant's ninety-one-year history.

**9:** *My first press conference as Miss America.*
**10:** *The historic final Miss America Top Five.*
**11:** *Being crowned by the reigning Miss America, Debbie Maffet, who was outspoken about it being time for a black woman to win the title.* **12:** *In less than five months, I went from Miss Greater Syracuse to Miss America!*
**13:** *With my Atlantic City police officer body-guards the morning after the pageant.*

# CHAPTER 3

*If you give your children the tools they need to survive, they can overcome anything—even a Miss America scandal.*

—HELEN WILLIAMS

This will all be over in a few minutes. Just get through the speech.

I had to be focused and composed. I repeated this to myself while taking some deep breaths. This was the biggest speech I would ever have to make in my lifetime.

It seemed like the world had turned out for my press conference. I knew there would be a lot of people, but this was pandemonium. Outside the Sheraton Manhattan, supporters lined the sidewalk, yelling: "Fight for the crown! Fight for the crown!"

I walked into the conference room flanked by Dennis Dowdell, my lawyer; and Ramon Hervey, my newly hired publicist. It was hot, noisy, and crammed with four hundred reporters and photographers from every newspaper, magazine, and television station—local, national, and international. I could feel the electricity and anticipation bounce around the room as photographers jockeyed for position, pushing and pulling and squeezing through the throng to get the perfect shot. I was blinded by the endless flashes from every direction.

*This is about me? Me? All this fuss and chaos is because of me? What? Everyone is acting crazy because of me? This is ridiculous.* I felt like I was the only sane person in a room filled with hundreds of Larrys, Curlys, and Moes.

The press was falling over one another. They were hurling insults when their angles were blocked. Now I could take a step back from the craziness and realize that this wasn't about me anymore. This was about an image that felt as removed from me as a stranger. I was observing a news story unfold. Two nights earlier, I watched Dan Rather report about me on *CBS Evening News*: "Vanessa Williams, the first black Miss America, was given seventy-two hours to resign. . . ."

It was surreal. Nine months earlier, I'd had my picture taken with Dan Rather. Now I'm an "important" news story—wedged right in between presidential coverage. I was superseding campaign stories! I stared in awe, thinking, *Whoa, this isn't me. I am watching this story just like everyone else, waiting to see what happens next.*

What *would* happen next?

That isn't to say it wasn't traumatic. It was all painful, embarrassing, and miserable. But distancing myself from the events helped me cope. It allowed me to do what I do best—execute. I had a speech I was going to deliver and I was going to do it perfectly. That was the task, the part, the monologue. I had to perform flawlessly without breaking down. I kept saying, "Just motor through the speech and move on." After all, that's what we Williamses do. We move on. We don't obsess. We don't cry in our rooms for days. We figure out what's next. We survive.

*Vanessa, now look what you've done.*

I read my speech. I stuck to the words written on the page.

Ramon and Dennis structured it beautifully and with no ambiguity.

*"The potential harm to the pageant, and the deep division that a bitter fight may cause, has convinced me that I must relinquish my title as Miss America. . . . "*

There were gasps and *no!s* along with the scribbling of notes and the pops of more and more flashbulbs.

There were a lot of people—even journalists, who were supposed to be impartial—who didn't want me to resign. My parents and friends thought I should fight. At first I felt the same way. As far as I was concerned, I'd done nothing wrong. I hadn't even thought about the photos when I signed on to the pageant; there's no clause that says, "No nude pictures." Looking back, I had signed a contract that had some guarantee that I hadn't committed any acts of moral turpitude. Had I committed such an act? I didn't think so.

The last few days had been absolutely insane. Three days earlier, July 20, I had been in Little Rock, Arkansas, at a corporate event for Gillette. I signed autographs at a local drugstore, where young black mothers and grandmothers lined up with their daughters and granddaughters, waiting to shake my hand and hug me as the first black Miss America.

"My little girls know they can do this because of you. Thank you for being a great role model," these mothers and grandmothers said.

I smiled, cringing inside. Would they still feel that way when the photos came out?

After the event, Midge Stevenson, one of the chaperones who'd been assigned to me after I'd won Miss America, raced toward me, looking very upset and confused. She had no idea what was going on.

"Your lawyer wants you to call him as soon as possible. He told me to tell you the news is about to break all over."

I called Dennis. He said that the press had just gotten advance copies of *Penthouse*'s September issue. He said I was on the cover standing next to George Burns (I'd had my photo taken with him at his eighty-eighth birthday party six months before).

The caption read: OH GOD, SHE'S NUDE!

This was 1984, so the news wasn't as lightning fast as it is today. Still, the story would be all over the place in a matter of hours. It would be the headline in the morning newspapers. I didn't know it then, but in just a little while I'd go from being the first black Miss America to, as the tabloids would proclaim: VANESSA THE UNDRESSA and MESS AMERICA.

That night, I attended a dinner with a bunch of Gillette executives. My blood pressure was through the roof. The news was still hours from breaking, so I smiled and acted like everything was fine. I had no appetite and moved my food around the plate but couldn't eat.

The next morning there was a knock on my door. The waiter who had brought breakfast to my hotel room told me that all the halls and exits were filled with reporters. Midge and I had to get out of there as fast as possible. Midge made a few phone calls. She arranged our flights and car service. But there was no way to sneak out of the hotel. We had to make a run for it.

"Just put your head down and keep moving," she said. "Don't stop for anything. Ignore the reporters."

There were no secret back exits, so we just blew through the crowd, right into the lobby, and raced to the awaiting car.

We were chased all the way to the airport by the paparazzi. A man with a long lens in a jeep was on our tail as we sped, changed lanes, took side streets. We tried to lose him, but he stayed next to us, shooting away. We drove onto the tarmac and climbed up the steps to the plane—without going through security. That was crazy VIP service!

It was an out-of-body experience.

Finally we boarded the TWA plane that would take us to St.

Louis, where we'd transfer to a flight heading for New York. Midge and I were settling in our first-class seats, trying to catch our breath.

"I don't believe this," I said as the plane took off.

A few minutes later, the flight attendant announced that we could unbuckle our seatbelts. Suddenly, the guy across from me pulled out a big video camera and turned it on: "Vanessa, how about a comment?" he said. He was part of a crew from CBS News that had somehow found out my itinerary—before I even knew what it was!

Midge put her hands in front of the lens. "Stop it," she yelled. I turned my head and faced the window.

The back of my head was an image that made it to the news that night.

Earlier that day, Albert Marks, the pageant chairman, had publicly requested my resignation within seventy-two hours. He didn't call me personally; he told every media outlet instead.

Should I resign? Should I let them dethrone me? Should I fight?

As much as I had seen Miss America as a temporary interruption to my goals, I had taken it seriously and given it my all. I'd done more appearances than any other Miss America in the pageant's history. I'd shown up at all the scheduled events, but I also did a lot of extra events in the black community. It was double-duty and exhausting. I felt like I'd done a really good job at it all. I had six weeks to go. Shouldn't I expect some loyalty from the pageant?

My father was furious. "They have no right to do this to you," he said. My father hated the injustice of it all. Fairness was a big part of his character. He believed they had no case against me. My mom agreed. They were my biggest champions and I didn't want to disappoint them. I wanted to fight, too, but was it worth it? It had become so much bigger than what it was. It had been transformed into a racial issue. Some black folks were saying, "Of course—she's black, so they're trying to get rid of her. We should have seen this coming. It's a conspiracy. They planned this all along."

After the press conference I went into hiding. I stayed with Dennis and his family just down the street from my parents' home, while hundreds of photographers and reporters were camped in front of my house. I was on practically every cover of the *Daily News* and the *New York Post* and other newspapers across the country.

One day, my dad picked me up from the Dowdells' to see how I was handling everything mentally. I remember his somber expression.

"Well, you really blew it, Ness," he said.

"I know, Dad."

There wasn't any rage or anger in his voice. It was almost matter-of-fact. My dad had been accustomed to my mistakes, but here was a mistake on a grand scale. Here was a mistake he and my mom had never in their wildest dreams imagined. There was almost a sense of humor to his words. He seemed to be telling me, *It's you and me against the world. We're in this together. But wow, this is big—even for you.*

I wouldn't have been able to power through this if it hadn't been for my parents. I never received any judgment from either of them. I never got "How could you?" "What were you thinking?"(Although I'm sure that's what they were thinking.) It was more like "Holy smokes—this is a doozy. How are we going to get through this? Well, no matter—we'll get through this!"

Dennis had hired a young black publicist from Los Angeles to help write my speech and plan my strategy. I was at the kitchen table when this handsome thirtyish man with a big, thick beard and curly hair introduced himself. He'd just taken the red-eye.

"I'm Ramon Hervey. I'm here to help you get through this," he said.

I thought, *Oh God, could he be any more L.A., with his Hawaiian shirt and Girbaud jeans?*

We sat down to work out a speech and decide whether or not I should resign or fight. We discussed it for hours. The lawyers had to incorporate their notes into the speech. Ramon said no matter what I decided, if I was holding a press conference, the speech would be the speech of my career.

"You have to say something that's meaningful. What you say in front of these journalists has to last forever," Ramon said. "No matter what you do for the rest of your life, this will be the most important speech you'll ever give."

He said I could be a footnote in history or I could tell the world that yes, I'm sorry this happened, but I'm not done. I'll be back. This is an embarrassing episode, but it doesn't define who I am and it doesn't take away from what I'll be. Once the dust settled, I would be seen for more than this episode. There were plenty of opportunities awaiting me. This experience was only a detour.

For hours and hours Ramon worked on the speech. We decided to hold the press conference on the final hour of the pageant's seventy-two-hour window. I couldn't eat or sleep. We went back and forth. Resign? Fight? No! Yes! When we had only about an hour until the conference, I decided to resign. Ramon quickly rewrote a few lines of the speech.

And here I was, motoring on: *"It has never been and it is not my desire to injure in any way the Miss America title or pageant."*

My reign had been filled with highs and lows. From the start it was never typical. I hadn't planned to win, so I never thought, *If I win, what happens next? What's my itinerary? What's expected of me? What will I be asked? Can I handle it?*

"Are you pro-choice? Pro ERA?" These were the rapid-fire questions reporters asked moments after I won.

"Yes. Yes," I answered. I wanted to establish myself as a modern woman who believed in equality, who believed in a woman's right to choose. I didn't have the standard Miss America patter down. My responses were considered pretty scandalous at the time. No Miss America had ever said anything like that before. But I was talking from my heart, not from a script. I was considered this extremely liberal New Yorker. But that's who I was at twenty.

"Name your favorite designers."

Designers? I wish I had money for designer clothes! Back then I worked and shopped at Discovery in Fashion on Route 117 in Bedford. There was a five-dollar rack and a ten-dollar rack. That was as designer as it got for me.

A foreign journalist explained, "If anyone asks you who your favorite designer is, always go for the Italian ones because they're the best."

Some people assumed I was from the "projects." I found out years later that the night I was crowned, Mary Ann Mobley, a former Miss America from Mississippi, had pulled my soon-to-be chaperone Midge Stevenson to the side and said, "Are you ready to go to Harlem now?" She knew nothing about me—she just thought that because I'm black, I must have been from a dangerous part of the inner city. Her husband, Gary Collins, was the host the year I won and sang to me "Miss America, You're Beautiful." That must have killed her.

The most heartbreaking part for me was the reaction from some black people. I had made history by toppling a barrier, but for some, winning wouldn't suffice. Some didn't think I was black enough. "She is light-skinned and light-eyed." "She's not from the hood." "She's not really black."

I come from a black mother and a black father. I have black grandparents on both sides. And that's who I am. I live the black experience every day because I'm a black woman born in America!

Then the next month, the New York *Daily News* ran a photo of Bruce and me having lunch at Maxwell's Plum—and the response was *"Oh my God! She has a white boyfriend!"* Here we go again with the barrage of angry phone calls and letters.

"You're a disgrace to your race," one letter sent to my parents' home said. "How can you represent black America with a white boyfriend? How can you screw a member of the white master race?"

I was invited to speak at Lincoln University, a small black college in Pennsylvania. During the question and answer period, one young brother, my age, asked why I didn't date black men. I did date black men. My first boyfriend, Joe, was black.

That taught me that you can't please everyone and no one really knows who you are through headlines, blurbs, and media sound bites.

The weekend I won had been a real whirlwind. I went from Atlantic City to New York City, and stayed in a suite at the Plaza Hotel, a legendary landmark, to kick off my first night on the road. On Monday, my parents; my brother, Chris; and I were interviewed by David Hartman on *Good Morning America*. I had a photo shoot in front of the Plaza by the big fountain with the statue of Pomona, the Roman goddess of orchards.

Then that Monday night, I was exhausted and ready to flop in my hotel room, so I turned on *The Tonight Show* to unwind. That's when I heard my name. Johnny Carson was talking about me in his monologue!

"Did you hear we have the first black Miss America? I bet you didn't know that Mr. T was one of the judges."

Wow—racist much? That hurt.

I stared at the television and thought, *That's so screwed up.* It was like a little punch to the gut. I wasn't stung by his comment, but it was a surprise. I called my mom. "Did you hear that?"

"Of course." My mom always has her radar on for comments like this. I knew she'd just put Johnny Carson on "the List"—it was her growing collection of people who'd done something unforgivable, at least in her eyes.

My parents' reaction to Johnny Carson was "Well, we can't shelter you anymore, Ness." I hadn't realized until then that I had lived in a nice bubble. I knew about racism, but I never really experienced it blatantly. My mom always told me that the color of my skin would cause some people to treat me differently, but now I was being reminded of it on a daily basis! My mom knew: "It's going to be rougher than we thought."

On *The Phil Donahue Show*, a woman in the audience stood up and stated: "You won because the lighting was different to make you look more white. You didn't look black at all."

*What? Are you kidding me?* I spoke as calmly as possible: "Did you actually watch the pageant? Did you hear me sing?"

There were also death threats—many of which I didn't know about because my parents didn't want me to spend my year in fear. But Mom would call me up and say, "Ness, be aware. There are people who are upset a black person won, and you have to be careful." My mother was not an alarmist. She'd say very calmly, "Listen, Vanessa, these are some of the phone calls we've gotten."

My parents refused to let Miss America rule their lives. They wouldn't change their phone number or become unlisted, so they'd get these crazy phone calls at the house. Stalkers would also knock on the door while I was out on the road. My dad would calmly talk to them on the porch and they'd eventually leave. Once, police picked up a disheveled looking man along Route 100, near my home. He called himself Mr. Bill and he'd come all the way from Chicago to visit me and harm my mom because she had hung up on him. The cops took him to the police station and then directly to a mental institution nearby.

My mother received death threats because she wouldn't put these crazy callers in touch with me. One caller wrote my mother saying he was saving money to come to Millwood and chop off her head. He'd send weekly updates on how much money was in his bank account: $484.15, $515.83, $520.75. It was insane—death threats on layaway.

When I made appearances in the South, I was always nervous. My mind flashed to my fellow Miss America contestant Deneen Graham, who was a brilliant ballerina. The year we competed, she'd been the first black Miss North Carolina. After she won, she came home to a cross burning on her lawn.

When I was in Selma, Alabama, an armed guard was stationed outside my hotel room. My chaperones would get calls to be on alert. They'd say to me, "When you go into your hotel room, do not open your door for anyone, even room service."

On top of the constant paranoia, there were times when I just wanted to walk away. I was asked to sing the national anthem at the Liberty Bowl in Memphis, forfeiting part of Christmas vacation at home. I told my dad I was too exhausted, too tired of worrying. I was close to quitting.

"I'm doing my best and there's so much negativity." I wasn't black enough for black people and I wasn't white enough for white people.

"Hey, this is your job. You can't quit," my dad said.

As rough as it was, the rewards were really amazing. After my triumphant runway strut, I returned to my room at Merv Griffin's Resorts Casino. The phone rang and my chaperone told me to pick up.

"Hello, Vanessa? This is President Reagan. Congratulations. This is a great thing for our nation," he said.

"Thank you very much, Mr. President." It was an amazing moment. During my reign, I would meet President Reagan twice— once at a state dinner and again at an Oval Office photo op.

I was starting my leap into celebrity. Soon after I won I was at an event where I met the hottest star of the time—Eddie Murphy. I was reduced to a giggling girl when he looked at me—I was and still am a huge fan. I was amazed that all of a sudden I was meeting and rubbing elbows with these people I'd always admired.

"Where do you live?" he asked.

"New York."

"Can I get your number?"

"Well, I'm on the road," I said. (There were no cell phones back then.)

He smiled at me. "So, you're *always* on the road? Don't you have any time off?"

"No." Did I really just say no to Eddie Murphy? But it was true, I had no time off. "I'm on the road every day in a new city for almost the entire year," I explained. "I fly in, do a gig, and fly out. I'm leaving for somewhere in the morning."

So I never went out with Eddie Murphy, although he'll always be the first big celebrity who asked for my number.

In October, I traveled to the White House for a state dinner with Karl Carstens, the president of West Germany (this was during the Cold War, when Germany was still divided into two countries). I wore my Miss America evening gown—the ivory Grecian dress that Vicki had bedazzled. A military guard escorted me up an elaborate stone staircase, and my name was announced along with the name of my handsome African-American soldier.

I was on my own—and nervous. In the receiving line before me was the legendary designer Halston and two of my dancing idols, Martha Graham and Ginger Rogers. Then it was my turn to shake hands and be introduced to Ronald and Nancy Reagan. They were such a regal couple. I couldn't believe how tiny Nancy was—she had the narrowest shoulders I'd ever seen. Next I shook hands with George and Barbara Bush, who took me under their wings and made sure I felt comfortable. "We're proud and excited for you," Barbara said.

During dinner, Sonny Jurgensen sat to my left and President

## VANESSA'S PRESIDENTIAL ENCOUNTERS

When I hung up my congratulatory phone call from **Ronald Reagan**, I had no idea that that was just the beginning of my presidential encounters, and that I would also get an official Oval Office visit.

Dining at the state dinner with President Reagan and Mrs. Reagan was a fairy-tale evening. You can't help but feel like you're in a movie when you're in their presence. They were elegant and glamorous. The president and Mrs. Reagan couldn't have been nicer.

At that same dinner I met **George Herbert Walker Bush**, who was vice president at the time. I will never forget how welcoming Vice President Bush and his wife, Barbara, were to me. They chatted with me and were loving, inclusive, and warm. I saw George again when he was president. I sang "Save the Best for Last" at the Ford Theatre for him.

By the time **George W. Bush** left the White House I felt that we were old friends. I'd attended five events during his two terms, and he'd always greet me with a warm smile. He even commented on one of my dates—who was twelve years younger than me—at Eunice Kennedy Shriver's White House birthday dinner: "Who's that young guy you brought?"

I took my mom to my first Kennedy Center Honors in 2005, where I sang for the honorees and President Bush. At the pre-show reception I told my mom, who didn't agree with his politics, "Keep your mouth closed—please!" You never know with my mom. But she shook his hand and kept moving. Whew! As far as I'm concerned, it's an honor to be invited. Respect the office . . . *always!*

I sang "Save the Best for Last" at **Bill Clinton**'s preinaugural concert. I also sang at a Very Special Christmas concert with the Special Olympics featured artists from the Christmas CDs the night before he was impeached. After he left office, Bill Clinton moved to Chappaqua, about a mile and a half away from my home. He called me right after my dad died and said he was so sorry to hear about it. He told me that even though his mother had been dead for many years, he still picked up the phone each Sunday to call her. (When I told my mom about his call, she said, "Why didn't he call me? He was my husband!")

I met **Barack Obama** on a Capitol Hill visit when I was campaigning for the Special Olympics. He had announced his candidacy and I had a brief sit-down in his office. After he won, I was one of the hosts for ABC's coverage of Obama's inaugural ball. I was there for the first dance, for which Beyoncé sang "At Last." I was just in awe of him and what he had accomplished. While I watched him dance, we all swooned at how passionately he loved his wife.

I met **Jimmy Carter**, my dad's favorite because of their similar childhoods, along with **Gerald Ford,** at Emory University in Atlanta, when I was invited as Miss America. I always had a particular fondness for Carter because my dad felt a kinship to him. He bought his autobiography and said to me, "His background is very similar to how I grew up." They both loved farming and had warm memories of their childhood. They had similar views on ecology and justice. They married strong women, were protective of their family, and were very open and honest.

Reagan was on my right. I had the best seat in the dining room. The conversation was a mix of sports and current events, but mostly the golden days of Hollywood. President Reagan would sigh, smile, and tell stories about the movies he'd been in. It was all unreal to a twenty-one-year-old.

But through it all, my mother's voice echoed in my head: "Whatever you do, get the president to sign your menu," she had told me.

"What? Now how am I going to do that?" was my response.

But Mom had been adamant. "It's something you'll always have. Keep a journal, too. Write this stuff down."

In between courses, before dessert, I said to President Reagan, "My mom will kill me if I don't get your autograph on the menu."

President Reagan chuckled. "Of course."

The things you do for Mom! At my next state dinner at the White House, I had President George W. Bush sign the menu along with the rest of the table.

That Thanksgiving I sang "New York, New York" from the top of the Big Apple float in the Macy's Day Parade. I waved to the crowd in my beige-and-ivory mink coat with a fox collar. (The coat wasn't a gift; Miss Americas received tremendous discounts.) Growing up, I'd watched that parade every year on television while helping prepare dinner, so to be actually on a float was a wonderful moment for me. (The other actress with the same name, Vanessa Williams, was mistakenly sent the check for my performance, but she graciously forwarded it to me.)

On the Fourth of July, I sang the national anthem on the USS *Intrepid*, the aircraft carrier. I took a helicopter to the event with legendary artist Ray Charles. I sang with Bob Hope on his college special from Syracuse University's Carrier Dome. I was serenaded by Ben Vereen at his concert in Texas. I had a guest appearance on *The Love Boat*, where I played myself as Miss America, along with three other past winners (Marian McKnight, Nancy Fleming, Jean Bartel). It was the first time I'd been to a television studio lot. The show was past its prime, but it was still a television staple. *The Love Boat* was such an iconic show. I smiled through every scene, I was so jacked.

And even though I had been nervous about sniper fire during my parade through historic Selma, Alabama, I was connected to the city's rich civil rights past. Now I had become a part of history. In Atlanta, I was introduced to Dorothy Height, a civil rights hero. Here I was, a symbol of opportunity, change, and tolerance. This was something I had never imagined.

Now, back to the abrupt ending—six weeks before my final walk.

I continued my speech. Ramon was next to me, looking over my shoulder as I read. His presence calmed me. With him there, I didn't feel so alone. I'd only known him for a few days, but we had gone through the fire already.

*"I feel at this time I could expend my energies in launching what I hope will be a successful career in the entertainment business."*

Looking back, would I do the pageant all over again? I know I'm supposed to say, "Yes, because it made me who I am today." But I don't always do or say what I'm supposed to do or say. And the truth is, I wouldn't do it again. But in this life, you don't get do-overs.

For years and years I'd walk into an audition or meeting and I could feel the judgment. They thought I was a beauty queen devoid of talent and intellect. Actually, not only a beauty queen—I was a scandalous Miss America. I was Vanessa the Undressa.

But I silently thought, *You have no idea who I am and what I can do. One day the dust will settle and you'll see what I am made of. You'll accept me for who I really am.*

What a difficult day for the family, but it was a relief, too. I knew once Vanessa made a decision, that would be the end of it. She doesn't dwell on things. I was very proud of the way she conducted herself.

There were hundreds of photographers on our lawn. It was driving me crazy. One day I said to myself, *I'm going to have a little fun.* I drove to the Maryknoll Sisters convent in Ossining, a few towns away. I watched as the paparazzi followed me. Then I stayed in the gift shop for a half hour. When I left, they followed me in their cars. The next day the papers wrote that Vanessa was hiding out with the nuns. I had a good laugh—Vanessa in a convent? It was a ridiculous thought. I had to think of things to do to take the seriousness out of the situation. We tried not to let this take over our lives—we didn't close the blinds and we came and went as we pleased, almost ignoring the photographers. But for my husband and Chris, it was just such a difficult, difficult time.

Then there was Ramon, who had come in as a professional. He's brilliant at what he does. But I thought, *Uh oh, Vanessa's going to fall for him.* She was leaning on him for support. He was her knight. Vanessa's always been a romantic—a bit too much of a romantic, if you ask me.

For a while I kept my mouth shut and just observed. I wanted to scream, "He's too old for you!" He was thirty-three—closer to my age than Vanessa's.

At first she told me they were just friends. Uh-huh. I don't look at my friends the way she was looking at Ramon!

There's always more to the story with Vanessa.

And of course, I was right.

When it comes to Vanessa, I'm almost always right.

*Now the Clintons are my neighbors!*

# CHAPTER 4

*You will never escape the scandal. It will always be there. Don't try to fight it, just accept that it will always be part of your story—a big part.*

—HELEN WILLIAMS

After living in my parents' home and hearing young high school kids scream out of their cars in front of the house, "Vanessa is a lesbian," I was ready to be on my own and move into the city. I fought for the scholarship money I was entitled to ($25,000 for winning the pageant, $4,000 for winning swimsuit and talent), got it, and decided to put it toward a condo in Manhattan.

Dennis, my attorney, had me meet a Realtor to start the search. Dennis was also managing my career, setting up record company meetings, working on endorsements for Royal Silk, tapping into all the interested parties. I also signed with International Creative Management, the top talent agency in New York. I saw a gorgeous one-bedroom apartment that I fell in love with on Sixtieth Street, kitty-corner to Lincoln Center. It had rounded balconies and plenty of light. I had enough for a down payment and couldn't wait to move in. Then the co-op board decided that they didn't want to sell the unit to me because of my notoriety. Crushed—and it still stings whenever I pass the Upper West Side building—I ended up renting an eastside apartment on Fifty-Fourth Street between First Avenue and Sutton Place. At $2,500 a month, it was very posh—a doorman building. I saw a one-bedroom and decided to upgrade to a bedroom with a dining nook on the nineteenth floor. I had no furniture at all—just my bed from my teenage bedroom, which was out of the question.

I was bed shopping at Macy's in midtown Manhattan when I heard the whispers. I'd gotten accustomed to being recognized, so I got a pair of fake reading glasses, hoping I would throw people off.

A black woman at a nearby counter saw me and said, "Boooo!"

There was no way to hide. What a disappointment I'd been to the black community—first a symbol of pride and triumph, now a symbol of shame.

I did nothing in response to the lady at the counter. I took the hit, pushed it down, and built up my armor. I wanted to disappear. Frankly, I wanted that woman to disappear! I bought my black lacquer platform bed (how eighties), escaped into the street, and went back to my apartment.

This wasn't the first time it had happened. Others had expressed disgust with me. But each time it hurt. I've had people sneer and spit on the street when I'd walk by. Some would say things like "You should be ashamed of yourself" and "What a disgrace!"

One time a parking attendant at a garage in New York City studied me and said with pity, "I hate to say it, but you look like Vanessa Williams." On the Millwood A&P parking lot some punks spray-painted VANESSA'S A LESBIAN.

But despite the heinous behavior of some, others reminded me that I wasn't alone. I got letters, phone calls, and telegrams from all over the world. There were lots of supporters.

Jesse Jackson called my dad and left me a message to "hold my head high." Sammy Davis Jr. took my parents aside at the *Motown Returns to the Apollo* televised concert and said, "I admire your daughter." He wrote down his phone number. "If you need any help, call me anytime. I'm here for you and her." Nikki Giovanni, the renowned black poet and writer, sent me a letter: "If I had a daughter, I would be more than delighted if she conducted herself as you have."

My parents received hundreds of supportive telegrams from friends and people I'd never met from all over the country, including the singer Lionel Richie; Cynthia Dwyer, a former hostage in Iran; and Laurie Lea Schaefer and the actress Lee Meriwether, both past Miss Americas. Lee, who has remained a friend and supporter ever since, sent me a beautiful letter that read as follows:

Dear Vanessa,

This is a sad and terrible time for you, I'm sure. But please! Please don't let this destroy you! You are a beautiful and talented young woman. USE THESE GIFTS! Remember, you will always be a Miss America and I will always be proud of you. Be brave and strong, my girl, as I know you can and must be.

Love, Your friend and sister,
*Lee Meriwether*

The local kids, some of whom I used to babysit, organized a Victory for Vanessa rally that paraded by my house. A bunch of the kids rang the doorbell and presented my mom with bouquets of flowers.

It was the only time I think she cried during the whole ordeal. I didn't witness it because I was hiding down the street, but it was captured in a photo that ran in all the local papers.

The scandal made the cover of newspapers and all the major

tabloids for two straight weeks. Even the *Daily Mirror* in Sydney, Australia, reported on the scandal with a cover story: BANNED BEAUTY. Most Europeans didn't get why this was such a big deal. *She was just* naked—*Americans are so uptight!*

For me, it seemed like an eternity in which I was the punch line to every late-night monologue. Joan Rivers, whom I adored and met on *The Tonight Show* during my reign, was particularly relentless. Just when I figured she'd exhausted every possible Vanessa Williams joke, she'd have a whole new slew of them. I had to learn not to take the attacks personally. "She's a tramp," she said over and over. (Ironically, "The Lady Is a Tramp" was one of the songs I sang on appearances as Miss America.)

Comedian Chris Rock attacked me on his HBO series *The Chris Rock Show*. Years later, I ran into him at the airport. He hemmed and hawed. I looked him right in the eye. "I heard what you said about me on your special."

He kind of stammered, "Yeah, well . . ." And that was the end of it. There was sort of this unspoken understanding. He was doing his job commenting on current events—and I was, unfortunately, the current event.

There were Vanessa jokes that went viral before there was such a thing as going viral: "Jesse Jackson is asking Vanessa Williams to run on his ticket. He knows she is the only one who can lick Bush."

UGH!

Larry Barton, the mayor of Talladega, Alabama, sent a letter demanding I return the key to the city he had presented to me when I served as grand marshal in their annual Christmas parade and sang the national anthem at the Talladega 500, the big NASCAR race. ". . . Miss Williams, you have permitted yourself to be exploited and disappointed thousands of Americans by your actions, but more important, you have disappointed God. . . . Please don't continue to waste your life. Ask God to forgive you, and ask him for guidance. . . ."

Of course my mother was furious. "You're not returning that key," she said. Then she sent him a letter: ". . . I can say with great certainty that Vanessa was an exemplary Miss America, and I could not, in view of that, justify returning your 'Key to the City.'"

In 1995, Mayor Barton was convicted and sent to prison on federal charges of defrauding the city of Talladega. (I guess it is okay to steal, but not undress!)

There were the calls to my childhood home and, of course, the barrage of hate mail. I was called the standard "Whore," "Pig," "Slut," but then there were some real doozies:

"You are worse than Hitler."

"In one fatal swoop, you pushed black people back to the time of slavery."

"You are part of Satan's chamber of horrors."

"You are a clone of every wicked thought and deed perpetuated upon mankind by Beelzebub."

Through it all, though, Ramon and I were getting closer. Bruce was in Syracuse and we were drifting apart. Ramon was commuting from Los Angeles to be with me. We spent time dating in New York, and traveled to the Bahamas and Fiji. He was my publicist and adviser, helping Dennis with business decisions as well. Ramon had spent years handling actors, musicians, and athletes, such as James Caan (whom I later worked with in the movie *Eraser*), Bette Midler, and baseball great Lou Brock. Ramon was established in the business and he knew so much. I could trust him because he had my best interest at heart.

He could also weed out the opportunists. The bullshit deals. He was convinced that, in time, I could get past the Miss America stigma and have the successful career I was meant to have.

I needed a break. All the other money offers had disappeared. I lost a ten-year promotional contract with Gillette. My Diet Coke commercial stopped airing. Kellogg's pulled off the shelves boxes of Corn Flakes with my picture on them. All in all, I lost about two million dollars in endorsements and countless other offers that would have come my way when I finished my reign.

There were a lot of insane offers, though. Cheesy shit. Ramon and I would laugh. I was asked to play the lead in a film called *Satan and Eve*.

No thanks.

*Thunder Women?*

No.

*Days and Night in Los Angeles?*

No.

Another producer approached me with the concept of starring in my own life story.

NO!

There were many fictional projects proposed just to get me into a meeting and check me out.

During my first year living in Manhattan, I got a call from Francine LeFrak, a producer friend. "Don't tell anyone, but Robert De Niro wants to discuss a possible project where you would costar in a Broadway musical with him." I was so excited. Starring with Robert De Niro? I didn't even know he sang and danced. But I thought it would be fantastic.

She told me she'd pick me up at my apartment and drive me to his place in Tribeca for the evening meeting. I wore a big, thick turtleneck sweater with a long knit tube skirt and boots. I was desperate to be taken seriously and hide any distractions. He was every bit a gentleman, offering me a drink while we sat on his deck under the downtown sky.

"You know, when I was young, I took nude photos, too," he told me. *Well, we have that in common*, I thought. But I really didn't want this meeting to revolve around my naked pictures.

"Tell me about the musical," I asked.

He was like, "Yeah, yeah, we'll get to it later. Tell me about yourself."

Details were vague. We sat there, making small talk. I tried to press him for more info: "What's the musical about? Who else are you considering?" He'd mentioned that it was an idea but nothing was definite yet. He was the ultimate in downtown cool.

But I also knew that my new flame, Ramon, was waiting for me in my apartment. There wasn't a musical. But if this was a chance to get hit on by De Niro, I choked.

"You should go into solo recording," Ramon said one day. "We could forge an identity, an image for you that way. If we fail, you can always go back to trying to make it as an actress. If we succeed, you'll have an image beyond being a dethroned Miss America. You'll have fans. You'll have a career. Don't wait around for the perfect movie role or the perfect Broadway show because it could take a long, long time, if it ever comes at all."

I kept saying, "It will happen. It will all work out. I just know it." My plan had always been to get on Broadway as soon as possible—not wait until I was established as a singer.

Ramon said I was in denial. I saw him as Eeyore, the pessimistic donkey in *Winnie the Pooh*.

"I'm not a pessimist—I'm a realist," he would respond. "Solo recording is your way to make a name for yourself on your terms."

But through all of this uncertainty, I could count on our growing love and I could handle my relationship and family on my own. I was the boss of me. And I was free to love.

Ramon admitted he had feelings for me, too. "But I don't date my clients," he said. Handling the Miss America debacle had been a great opportunity for him, as he was already well-known as a celebrity publicist in Los Angeles. But this scandal had put him on everyone's radar.

"Everything I do right now will come under a microscope," he said. "If I start dating my client, I'll lose all credibility."

I understood. Here was this older guy who had been hired to

help a twenty-one-year-old woman in the biggest crisis of her life. It was all the clichés—hero and victim; rescuer and rescued.

But I didn't care. He was smart, handsome, sophisticated, warm, and kind. He was independent, strong, and had a relaxed way about him, like he didn't have to prove anything to anyone. And he could cook. He seemed perfect.

But my mother wasn't so easily impressed.

My mother is this force. When she disapproves, you can see it on her face. Her eyes blaze. She gives this icy stare. We all call it "the Look." She might not say anything, but you can feel the force. It can fill a room. It's so powerful that when I was cast in *Ugly Betty*, I used "the Look" for my character, Wilhelmina. The show's writers eventually included it in the script—*Wilhelmina gives the Look*. It was an inside joke with friends and family: "Wilhelmina *is* your mom!"

Mom liked Ramon and respected the public relations work he'd done for us. But she didn't like us as a couple. He knew it. I knew it. I wanted my mom to like him. I felt she didn't approve of my boyfriend Bruce because he was white. Subconsciously I was thinking, *Ramon's a black man—are you happy now, Mom? Doesn't he remind you a bit of dad—a bearded Libra with a kind nature?* Plus he saved the day; how could she not like him?

But with Mom there was always a problem, always a complaint. "He's way too old for you. You're twenty-one—he's thirty-three. You're at different places in life."

Falling in love with Ramon was the perfect distraction from all the mayhem in my life. It was a great escape to be excited about someone. I could focus on our relationship instead of the impending legal battle with *Penthouse*, the media attention, the late-night television jokes. Who cares about any of that when you're newly in love? We tried to keep it quiet. I wasn't sure what I was doing and neither was Ramon. He was still in Los Angeles, so our relationship was long-distance. We took it slowly. We only told a handful of friends. When he visited, we stayed in, afraid of what the press would write if they found out we were a couple.

I was trying to establish as normal a life in Manhattan as possible. I was like any newcomer to the city. I spent my days furniture shopping. I painted and wallpapered the place myself. I'd bus it across town to Broadway Dance Center and take jazz class with Frank Hatchett, a dancing legend. From the outside, it looked like I was living the life. I had this ridiculously expensive apartment. I walked around Manhattan in the mink coat I'd worn at the Macy's Day Parade. But at times, I didn't even have taxi money.

Then one day it seemed like everything might begin to fall in place.

Paul Martins, my theater agent at ICM, told me that Mike Nichols, the famous stage and film director (*The Graduate*, *Who's Afraid of Virginia Woolf?*), wanted me to audition to replace model-actress-icon Twiggy in *My One and Only*, a musical based on George and Ira Gershwin's *Funny Face*, a period piece set in 1927.

Perfect. Right up my alley! I'd get to showcase all my talents— singing, dancing, and acting—and I'd learn to tap with legendary choreographer Tommy Tune. Finally I was being taken seriously— and by one of the most successful directors out there. I knew this part—Edith Herbert, a former English Channel swimmer living in the Jazz Age—was perfect for me.

I met Mike Nichols at the St. James Theater. A few days before, Tommy Tune, who costarred in the musical, had taught me the tap dance routines at a studio. For the last few days, I'd practiced my ass off. I was more than ready. This part had my name on it.

My audition was flawless. I sang. I danced. I kicked higher than ever. I connected with Tommy Tune on stage. I knew I nailed it and I could tell that Tommy Tune and Mike Nichols were really happy with my performance.

"That was great, perfect," Mike said. "You're the real thing and we want you in this play. As far as we're concerned, the part is yours. We just have to run it by Lenora ["Lee"] Gershwin, who is executive producer of the show."

I was ecstatic. Finally, it was happening, just like I knew it would. I was on my way to being a Broadway star! *Broadway, here I come.*

Mike Nichols called me the next day. "I have some bad news."

He told me that he had just met with Lee Gershwin, the late Ira Gershwin's wife, at her suite at the Regency Hotel in midtown. "We told Lee we'd found a really exciting girl who sings great, dances great, and is gorgeous—her name is Vanessa Williams. She said 'Well, you boys are so talented. So whatever you want is fine with me.' And then the minute we got to the lobby, her lawyer, who was in the meeting with us, received a call at the desk. It was Lee. She told him, 'I just want it to be clear: I don't want that whore in my play.' I'm devastated by this, Vanessa, but there's nothing I can do. She has the final say."

That was the moment it really hit me.

All my life, Broadway had seemed like this attainable goal. It was only a train ride, an audition away. I'd watch the commercials, see the shows, study the performers, and think, *I have the talent. I can do this. This is possible.* I'd written "See you on Broadway" next to my high school yearbook photo.

I thought, *Okay, now I get it. This has nothing to do with talent. This is going to be harder than I ever imagined. This Miss America thing is going to be a huge, huge obstacle.*

I was upset. I was frustrated. But I didn't want to kill myself, as was reported. I look back at stories and headlines written about me at the time. They'd say things like VANESSA'S DARK DAYS or VANESSA'S HIT ROCK BOTTOM. I knew it would be tough, but I also never doubted I would succeed. When you know this, you don't have dark days, you don't hit rock bottom. You just have days when you want to scream at people: "You have no idea what I can do!"

• • •

Besides working on my career, I was also suing Bob Guccione, the publisher and founder of *Penthouse,* for publishing my nude photos without a signed release from me. His response? He published more of them in the November issue, with plans to publish another round of photos (Gregg Whitman's) in January. It was a game to him. He figured he had all the money in the world, and I posed no threat to him.

There were endless depositions at his lawyers' offices as we prepared for trial. His attorneys were ruthless and their questions were condescending.

"Oh, you were a musical theater major? Did you weave baskets there, too? Oh, you took modern dance AND ballet. WOW!"

Guccione's lawyers and his whole crew were so vile. I couldn't stand them. I answered each question as calmly as possible: "Yes, I was a musical theater major. Modern dance and ballet were part of the curriculum."

They just bombarded me with more silly questions in the middle of my answers. They'd bring up past jobs and past relationships. Was this supposed to break me? Make me throw in the towel and say, "I quit"? These lawyers may have been experts at making people feel insignificant and foolish, but they couldn't get me.

My lawyers warned me that there were no secrets they wouldn't be able to unearth. Bob Guccione had endless resources. The trial could drag on forever. My parents, both elementary schoolteachers, were paying most of my bills. They wanted me to fight, but they couldn't afford it. I hated asking for their funds—especially to pay for my mistakes.

My mom said, "It will cost us more money than we have. We don't have Guccione money. We're prepared to do it. But I think he's a slimebag and not worth the time."

My legal team laid it out. "Anything you've ever done will come up in a trial. And the trial will be very public. Everything you say will be splashed all over the tabloids. They'll dig into every aspect of your personal life."

More headlines? More judgment? I wanted it to be over. What were we really winning anyway? I'd just be getting publicity for all the wrong reasons.

I thought, *I'm done. My life is finally not a circus right now. So who needs this?*

Broadway wasn't ready for me yet, but I'd be back. I knew it. Once the dust settled, I'd be on stage. I performed in a lively off-Broadway show, *One Man Band*, and kept my dream alive. But I was ready for more.

I decided that I'd take Ramon's advice—try a solo recording career—and one day find my way back to Broadway. Ramon had been right. As much as I tried, I couldn't plan every aspect of my career. Meryl Streep's footsteps were not mine. I had to find my path.

I had to surrender to the unknown.

---

I've always had "my List." Ness will say I remember every negative comment that's ever been said by friends, acquaintances, the media. I'd like to say I can forgive. But I can never forget. It's just not my nature. I can't do it. Maybe that means I'm not really forgiving anyone, either.

I think of the List more as my being somewhat of a mama bear protecting her cubs. Before Vanessa became Miss America, the List was manageable. Then the scandal broke out and the List took on a life of its own. I would constantly say, "That person's on my List."

Here's a sampling.

# MY LIST

**JOAN RIVERS.** I know her shtick can be cutting and sarcastic. But she was downright cruel to Vanessa, and she made me furious. I fumed and glared at the television. I accepted that she is a comedian and jokes would be told, but I still thought there would be a bit of sensitivity in her comments because she is also the mother of a daughter. It was naive of me, but the jokes did hurt.

**TONY BROWN.** I couldn't stand him. I loathed him. He had a local radio show and is the host of PBS's *Tony Brown's Journal.* He's supposed to be this "civil rights crusader"—but to me, he isn't at all. He's a mean-spirited, hypocritical person with a cable show. It seemed to me that he had a big problem with my light-skinned black daughter. Vanessa was a target of his hate from the beginning. Then when the pictures came out, he spent weeks and weeks just destroying her, calling her names. I stopped listening. He's probably a contributing factor to why I have high blood pressure.

**THE PAGEANT PEOPLE.** It really infuriated me that Vanessa was Miss America for nearly eleven months and when the scandal broke, pageant officials had her chaperone drop her off at the front door, and we never heard from anyone again. It was like they couldn't get rid of her fast enough. They just wiped their hands of her because they felt she was no longer of any value to them. I was optimistic for a while. I really thought they would call or make some contact. When they didn't, I had no choice but to put them on the List.

**THE WOMEN OF *THE VIEW*.** A few years ago Vanessa produced and starred in a TV movie, *The Courage to Love.* She played a nun. *The View* discussion centered on questioning Vanessa's producing and starring in a story about a nun after what she did. As her mom I went into protective mode. So I wrote a letter to the show expressing my feelings about what I perceived to be an unfair criticism. The response I received was the standard acknowledgment postcard—but I felt better.

*My first apartment on the eastside. Moving on up!*

PART TWO

# THE
# RIGHT STUFF

# CHAPTER 5

I was twenty-three and scared when I found out I was pregnant. I didn't think I had a maternal instinct in my body. I had never babysat or changed a diaper. I'd never even been around little children. When it came to motherhood, I didn't have a role model to imitate. I wasn't sure if I would be able to be a good mother.

But Milton assured me I'd be a natural. He'd grown up around children of all ages. He knew how to change diapers, fix a bottle, and put a baby to sleep. It would be easy, he promised.

I had my doubts.

Vanessa was born ten days late on March 18, 1963, at 11:28 A.M., weighing seven pounds seven ounces, and measuring twenty inches. She was beautiful, with brown hair and smoky blue eyes. We named her Vanessa Lynne for two reasons: *Vanessa* is an opera by Samuel Barber, one of my favorite composers; and Vanessa means *butterfly* in Greek. I have always loved butterflies—they're so graceful and they come in such a wonderful assortment of colors. (I may get a butterfly tattoo one of these days.)

I was lucky—Vanessa was a happy and healthy baby. She'd been easy before she was born—I didn't have morning sickness or strange cravings. When I was in labor, I only had some lower back pain—and I was only in labor for about two hours.

But she let out this fierce cry when she was hungry or wet or wanted something that we couldn't figure out. Once she got going, she was almost impossible to stop. Even as a baby she wanted everyone to notice her. I discovered that if I set her in her playpen in the middle of a room of people, she'd quiet down. She loved to be around people.

One time a reporter said, "Tell me something about Vanessa that no one knows." So I said, "Well, she used to suck her thumb." He wanted some dirt, but that's what I gave him. She was a thumb sucker; and we couldn't get her to stop. I sewed little mitts and put them on her hand, but she'd just pull each of them off and get at that thumb. I dipped her finger in a bitter solution, but she didn't mind the taste—she just wanted to get at that thumb. Finally, when it was time to go to preschool, she stopped.

Here's another thing no one knows about Vanessa: As a baby she'd wail whenever the theme song from *Lassie* came on the television. Milton and I couldn't figure it out. We'd look at each other and ask, "What is bothering her so much?" Was she afraid of the big dog? Or did the music make her very sad?

Even then, there were some things about Vanessa that we just couldn't figure out.

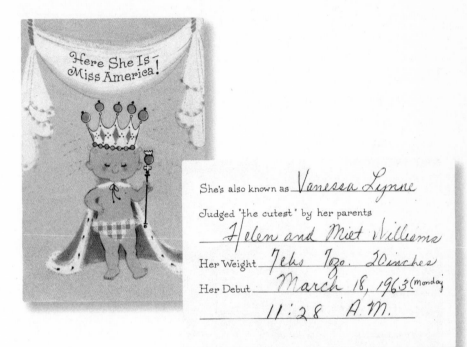

Here She Is!
Miss America!

She's also known as *Vanessa Lynne*

Judged "the cutest" by her parents

*Helen and Miet Williams*

Her Weight *7 lbs. 7 oz. 20 inches*

Her Debut *March 18, 1963 (monday)*

*11:28 A.M.*

# CHAPTER

# 6

*If you're going to run away from home, that's fine—just make sure you don't cross the street when you do!*

—HELEN WILLIAMS

When I close my eyes and think about my childhood, I can hear its sound track:

Mom's downstairs in the family room at the baby grand piano, ordering students to play their scales. While my dad—a one-man woodwind and brass ensemble—is upstairs teaching trumpet or clarinet or saxophone or French horn or oboe to a neighborhood kid. In between lessons, he picks up his flute and the sounds of Bach's Badinerie from Overture no. 2 in B Minor flood our raised ranch home.

Children counting out measures—*ta, ta, ti, ti, ta.* The tinkling of piano keys. The ticking of a metronome. Saxes playing in unison (my dad always played with his students).

Some people have comfort foods. I have comfort sounds.

Ever since I can remember, music was everywhere, all the time.

It was inescapable. Music is part of my DNA—both my parents were music teachers, singers, and dancers. When I was a baby, Mom and Dad would take me to their Westchester Baroque Chorus rehearsals. I'd cry unless they plopped me in the playpen in the middle of the room—I loved being around people, Mom would say. I'd coo along to their voices.

My mom told me that one time while they were singing Handel or Bach, I hit a really high note in perfect pitch, on key. At first they thought it was an organ key that got stuck. The group paused: *Did she really do that?*

At home, when someone wasn't playing an instrument, the stereo was on. Mom loves show tunes—*The Sound of Music, Purlie, My Fair Lady.* Some of her favorite singers are Roberta Flack, Frank Sinatra, Nat King Cole, Ella Fitzgerald, and Rosemary Clooney. Dad had eclectic tastes—he would listen to Tito Puente, Mongo Santamaria, Bill Withers, John Coltrane, the Beatles, the Temptations, the Staple Singers, gospel, classical, and salsa. He also loved big brass ensembles. Last year, at my daughter Jillian's graduation, I recognized a piece Dad listened to all the time when I was a child. I smiled and thought, *Even though he's not with us anymore, he's here. I can feel him through this music.*

I'd soak in all of the music—jazz, pop, classical, show tunes—my parents played in the living room. But in my bedroom I would listen to the pop station WABC on my little yellow transistor radio. This was at a time before music became compartmentalized, and I would hear all kinds—Elton John, Marvin Gaye, Chaka Khan, Teddy Pendergrass, Fleetwood Mac. I'd also listen to the Jackson 5's *ABC*—the first album I ever bought. Everyone had that one. I loved every song and I would belt out the lyrics as I danced around my pale pink wallpapered room or jumped on my canopied bed.

Michael Jackson was my favorite singer and my first crush. He was so young and so talented. I drew a heart around his face on the back of the album cover. I met him years later at Quincy Jones's fifty-fourth birthday party in 1987. Ramon had worked with the Jackson family years before. I shook Michael's hand. He seemed so slight, so fragile, so soft-spoken. What a difference between the childhood idol who I wanted to kiss and the man I just wanted to give a big, tender hug.

Growing up, we had a young girl, Diana, watch us before my mom got home from school. Then when I got older, I was a latch-key kid. The school bus dropped my brother, Chris, and me off right in front of the house. We'd head inside, race into the kitchen, and devour Hostess Fruit Pies, Ding Dongs, or Sno Balls (living just a few miles from the Hostess and Entenmann's factories had its benefits—my dad would pick up the treats on his way home from school) and wash them down with Yoo-Hoo, grape soda, or milk. We'd play outside for a while and then I'd head to my room, flop on my white chiffon canopied bed, and do homework.

"Don't answer the door. Don't pick up the phone. Don't talk to anyone," Mom would tell us. Mom was always on edge, always suspicious, always expecting the worst.

But we weren't latchkey kids for very long. Since Mom and Dad were schoolteachers just a few towns away from where we lived (Mom in Ossining, Dad in Elmsford), they'd usually be home a little while after we were. Then they'd start their second jobs—teaching music to local children. Our front door was always unlocked and there was always a car or two waiting in the driveway. My dad also taught students at their houses before he'd come home.

When I finished my homework, I'd throw open the screen door and run outside to ride my bike with Maura, my neighbor. We'd head to Elmer's, the local five-and-dime, for some rock candy. Or I'd play tag or hide-and-seek with the neighbors or ride on our whirl-igig.

As the light dimmed, Mom would call us in for dinner. We'd sit around the table, discussing the events of the day. Mom would tell us some funny stories about the kids she taught at Claremont Elementary. Sometimes Dad would pull out black-history flash cards. In between forkfuls of roast chicken or mac and cheese (our favorites), Dad would quiz Chris and me on icons and pioneers like Martin Luther King Jr., Rosa Parks, Malcolm X, Harriet Tubman, and Mary McLeod Bethune.

My parents would say, "We may be one of the only black families in the area—but we aren't going to forget who we are." They never stopped teaching!

My parents were hell-bent on making us as independent as possible, as young as possible. Since we were practically toddlers, we could tie our shoes and make our beds. My mom was so far from being a helicopter mom (and so am I). She believed that children needed to figure things out on their own without a mom hovering over them, waiting to pounce. If I asked my mom for something, she'd tell me to get it. If I ran out of clean clothes, she'd point to the washing machine.

When I was older and learning to drive, my father taught me how to change a tire. He handed me a jack and some lug nuts. "I don't ever want you to be in a situation where you feel helpless," he said. Years later, when I was driving home from Syracuse University, I had a blowout and was able to change the tire all by myself. I could still do it today if I had to.

Mom and Dad also wanted me to know how to do everything the correct way. Mom taught me how to properly set the table. She'd hold both hands out in front with the palms facing each other. Then using the tips of her thumb and forefinger, she'd make circles with her fingers. "Your left hand makes a *b* and your right hand makes a *d*." She said this was the way I could remember that the bread goes on the left and the drink goes on the right.

She'd grab my hand and show me how to shake it firmly while

## HELEN'S REASONS FOR WHY CHILDREN SHOULD PLAY AN INSTRUMENT

- Children develop a sense of stick-to-it-iveness in order to master an instrument.
- Children learn a skill they will have for the rest of their lives.
- Children understand how to work with a group in a way that's different from all other activities. They are a piece of a puzzle, all working toward a common goal.
- Children who play instruments tend to do better academically because they're better organized.

looking directly into the person's eyes. "People judge you on these things," she'd explain. "You want to always make a good first impression."

After dinner we'd load the dishwasher. Then music would fill the house all over again. Chris and I would have to practice our instruments. While I played French horn, Chris played piano. When we were finished, I would take over the piano and Chris would pick up his oboe. Dad taught us the instruments, but as we improved, Mom picked up the piano lessons because she was an excellent pianist and organist.

Sometimes, however, I just wanted to head into the living room and watch TV—*The Brady Bunch, I Dream of Jeannie, Bewitched, Good Times*, and *Sanford and Son* were some of my favorites. But since the fourth grade, I've had to play two instruments. No questions. It was a Williams family rule that sometimes drove me crazy.

Once, I ran away from home to escape practicing the piano. I'd had enough. I took a few of my stuffed animals and my sleeping bag and announced that I was leaving for good.

"That's fine. Just don't cross the street," Mom had said. I hid in the woods behind the house until it started getting dark and I began hearing strange animal sounds. Then I ran back home, deciding it was easier to practice than to escape.

While the weekdays were filled with music, the weekends had a much different sound—the whir of a cement mixer, the high pitch of a drill, the banging of a hammer, the buzzing of a saw. Dad was constantly building, fixing, renovating, plowing, creating. My dad was a Renaissance man, an inventor—he even built me a car seat before there were such things as car seats. He sawed off the legs of an old high chair and strapped the contraption in between the driver's and passenger's seats of our blue Ford Econoline van. Then we'd head off on road trips—to our cabin (that he built) in the Poconos, or to visit relatives in Buffalo or Baltimore.

My mom loved nice things for her home and my dad would love to build them for her. My childhood home was a brick-and-mortar love letter to my mother. If my mom casually mentioned, "Oh, I'd love a bigger deck," my dad would say, "Okay," and he'd start planning that day. He'd write up the plans and draw sketches. He had a bunch of how-to books on the bookshelf (which he built, of course), and he would figure everything out and do it himself. For a while he and a teaching buddy had a deck-building company called Dexterity, but he preferred home projects. He loved being home and around his family. In the summertime, when he was off from school, he was always working around the house on some project.

When I was a toddler, my mom said, "Wouldn't it be nice to have a pool?" The next day, Dad bought a book on how to build a pool. He spent the winter months devouring every aspect of pool construction. When the earth thawed in the spring, he began excavating. By summer the Williams family had a beautiful vinyl-lined inground swimming pool—the only one in the neighborhood. My dad did everything. He never stopped working.

My mom would call the house I grew up in "your dad's house," because the house we moved into and the house it became were two different places. Dad blew out the back and added a den. He extended the upstairs porch. He poured concrete and put in a driveway. He built the deck. He built ramps and retaining walls. The house became my dad's artistic vision.

Our garage was the stuff of legends—at least in our small town. We lived right on Route 100, which is a major connecting street, and people all over town would idle their cars when they passed to take a look inside dad's garage. It was stacked floor to ceiling with Dad's tools, supplies, and equipment. There was no room to park a car.

While my mom, Chris, and I saw complete chaos, my dad saw methodical organization. He could find whatever he needed. He was the guy all the neighbors went to for tools, advice, and help. When I got older and had a home of my own, I never ever had to call a handyman. I'd just call Dad with my problems—a noisy furnace, a leak, an air conditioner that wouldn't work. He'd be right over and he'd fix it.

If you asked my mom to describe Dad, she'd say he was a "very serious man." It's funny because I never thought of him as serious at all. He's the man who lit up a room when he walked in and always laughed louder and longer than anyone else. But my mom had such a different take on him.

The other day, I was driving along Mulholland in Los Angeles and I saw pant legs sticking out from underneath a car. I got a lump in my throat because it reminded me so much of my dad. If Dad wasn't building or gardening, he was repairing a car. He had the brain of an engineer, mechanic, and nutty professor. People would marvel at his mechanical skills. He could take an engine apart, spread it out on the sidewalk, and put it back together.

One time he bought an old red Fiat 128. It wasn't unique enough, so he bought a compressor and then turned the garage into an auto body shop. He transformed the Fiat into a silver sports machine with a groovy racing stripe down the side. I learned how to drive in that car (stick shift on the dirt road behind a big pond at Gedney Park).

When I picture my dad, he's always wearing work boots, work pants, and a T-shirt. He's always sweaty. He always has a handkerchief in his pocket, and he takes it out and wipes his brow. He had calloused hands that he'd wash the dirt from in the utility sink next to the washer and dryer. On top of the sink he always had a tin with grease remover. He would scrub his hands until he'd clean off all the oil from the cars, or the dirt from the garden that was wedged underneath his fingernails. The smells of paint or freshly sawed wood are the smells of my father.

If my dad and mom were working, so were Chris and I. We couldn't just plop down in front of the television and watch cartoons all day. (Although sometimes I wished I could!) When we were little, we'd hand our dad tools—wrenches, screws, hammers—while he worked. As we got older, we'd paint, mow the lawn, pull weeds from the garden, dig, plant. We had our regular chores (I'd clean the bathrooms; Chris vacuumed) as well as washing clothes, sewing, ironing, but we were also expected to help out with the bigger family projects. And there always seemed to be big family projects.

(This sense of work ethic and responsibility is probably the reason why I hate being "handled." I absolutely hate it. People hovering around me and speaking for me irks me. I'd rather do it myself than be disappointed by someone else doing it. Just give me my space, let me take care of it, and I'm happy.)

• • •

My dad loved gardening. He grew up in Oyster Bay on Long Island, New York, which was a very rural farming community. My dad talked about his childhood as being very free, full of exploring the woods as well as the mansions along the Gold Coast. As a child, he spent his free time gardening, picking beans, and irrigating crops.

At Oyster Bay High School on Long Island, he was very conflicted. Should he be a musician or a farmer? He played the alto saxophone and was part of the marching band. Mr. Luckenbill, his teacher, told him, "Be a musician. You're really talented. Go to SUNY Fredonia and study music."

But part of Dad always remained a farmer. He built a greenhouse that was lined with clay pots of all sizes. He'd plant seeds. Then he'd transfer the shoots to the huge garden where he had two-foot-by-two-foot patches fenced off for his fruits and vegetables. Dad grew everything—lettuce, corn, beans, beets, potatoes, squash, tomatoes, pumpkins, zucchini. He never used pesticides. Dad was eco-friendly before anyone knew the phrase. He was really ahead of his time.

During the summer, I'd pick tomatoes from the garden, slice them up, shake on some salt and pepper, toast some bread, and make the most delicious sandwiches. At the end of the summer, I'd set up a vegetable stand in front of the house where I'd sell zucchini and tomatoes for five cents each. Then I'd ride my bike to Elmer's and spend my money on rock candy, Bazooka bubble gum, and my all-time favorite, Atomic FireBalls.

I was always trying to make money, whether it was selling vegetables, babysitting, or hawking Avon cosmetics door-to-door as a junior sales rep. I loved to spend my money on clothes. We might be working on a family project on a Saturday, but Mom and I would escape for a few hours to shop. That was our special time together. My mom loves to shop for bargains, and even today I like to get good deals.

We shopped at all the discount stores—Caldor, Korvette's, Alexander's, and Master's. I always got the discount version of whatever was hot. One year, everybody had navy peacoats. I got my Master's version—I have no idea who the designer was. I didn't care that it wasn't the "real" thing. I had it and rocked it. Who knew the difference? I bought my painter's pants and overalls there, too. Everyone wore Frye boots, but I had my knockoffs.

Then there was my childhood lunchbox. All of my friends had cute little lunchboxes with images of the Partridge Family or the Monkees. Dad bought me a big metal construction worker's–style lunchbox. Horrible, I thought. Dad caught me sulking and handed me a bag of big daisy stickers.

"Ness, make it your own. Dare to be different," he said.

If I wanted something extra, I had to buy it. When I was in about seventh grade, I saved up money to buy a purple ten-speed Fuji Special Tourer bike.

My dad said, "I'll pay for half of it and then you can pay me back when you make the money doing chores and babysitting." My dad loved contracts. He'd have me sign a piece of paper promising to pay back however much I owed him. There were always charts on the refrigerator, detailing how much I had paid and how much I still owed.

Until I was twelve, Dad read to me every night. My childhood home was crammed with books. Dad would read anything and everything and then he'd read them to me. When I was little, it was the typical stuff—fairy tales, Dr. Seuss, nursery rhymes. My dad was always a great storyteller. He'd read a story and act it out with different voices—Donald Duck, Porky Pig, whoever. He'd make everything come alive. He'd sing and change expressions and make you feel like you were living the story. He was like the Danny Kaye of Millwood. If I had friends over, he'd be in the corner with a book surrounded by kids. He'd say, "Let me tell you the story of the Ugly Duckling"—and then all these characters would emerge from him.

As I got older, Dad would read me psychology books such as *I'm OK-You're OK, Psycho-Cybernetics,* and *What Do You Say After You Say Hello?: The Psychology of Human Destiny.* My father was fascinated with psychology. The bookshelf over my parents' bed was filled with psychology books. He devoured them all. I remember noticing a book called something like *The Frigid Woman,* and I thought, *Hint, hint, MOM!*

After he'd read to me, we'd pray together. When I was a toddler, my dad taught me how to pray and I still recite the same prayer every night before I go to bed: "Now I lay me down to sleep . . ." But Dad didn't say, "If I die before I wake." He had a different version:

*"Now I lay me down to sleep. I pray the Lord my soul to keep. May love guard me through the night and wake me with the morning light. Help me do the things we should, to be to others kind and good. In all we do and all we say, to grow more loving every day."*

I could talk to Dad about anything—school, friends, feelings. When I got older and was away at school or living on my own, I'd call the house and be like, "Hi, Mom, how are you? Is Dad home? Can I speak to Dad?" He was always the easier person to talk to. I felt I had a really strong connection with him. I'm sure Mom felt a little bit left out because we were so close. But when I look back, I think, *Wow, what a great father-daughter relationship I had.*

One night when I was little, Dad finished reading a fairy tale to me and I turned to him and asked, "Daddy, why doesn't Mommy love me? Why doesn't she hug me?"

He looked at me and smiled. Then he spoke softly and slowly. "Well, Mommy had a really hard time growing up. The people who raised her really treated her badly. They gave her beatings. It's hard for her to show love, but that doesn't mean she doesn't love you. She loves you very much."

Sometimes I wasn't sure my mother loved me, but my dad explained my mother's behavior in such a loving way that I could understand why she had problems showing affection. There were times I couldn't stand my mother, but I learned early on that my mother had—I don't want to say issues—but yes, she had issues! And even though it took a lot of work, my father was probably the only person who understood my mom—and he tried to help me understand her.

My dad had a lot of patience. He could spend countless hours teaching, explaining, and showing. I marvel at the patience he had. I can't remember him snapping at us, ever.

My mom told me that when I was little, my dad spanked me once. For what? No one remembers. I have no recollection of this at all. I cried really hard and it just ripped him. He said he would never do it again—and he never did. He was such a caring, sensitive man.

One time I came home from my friend's house, and I just blurted out, "Charlotte's mom made the best hamburgers in the world! They were fried in butter and just fabulous."

My dad took me aside and said, "You know, your mom's burgers are really good, too—so I would definitely mention that to her." We had a very sensitive household, but my mom was extremely sensitive, and my dad definitely took care of her feelings, her moods. He knew that she'd interpret my comment as an insult to her cooking, even though I didn't mean it that way. I was just a kid who'd eaten a really good burger.

My parents never argued in front of us. If there was a disagreement or some tension, they'd tell Chris and me to go outside and play on the swings or in the sandbox. But this rarely ever happened. Usually when it did, it was Mom who was upset and she'd go in her bedroom and close the door. It was never dramatic. She'd just disappear and my father would go talk to her and all would be resolved. There were never big screaming fits. I grew up in a very calm, Zen-like household.

My mom will say my dad is the only person who could have put up with her. She knows she's a lot to handle, and she enjoys it. It's not like she's unaware of her strengths. If my dad's Danny Kaye, my mom's Joan Collins. She loves drama. She loves to be the center of attention. My mother is a spitfire, and she tells it like it is—she doesn't sugarcoat the truth. Ever.

When I was about eight and riding the bus home from Westorchard Elementary, a girl and her brother called me "nigger" to my face. I had no idea what the word meant, but I knew it was ugly because they had said it with such venom. When I got home, I told my mother what had happened and then asked, "What does that mean?"

I'm sure this was a moment my mother knew would one day come. She'd battled racism her entire life. "There are some people who have a problem with the color of our skin, so you're going to have to be better than everybody else to be accepted as an equal."

When I think back to that incident, I'd have to say that the words my mother spoke to me had much more of an impact than what

## HELEN ON RACISM

I knew someday Vanessa would be called that word. I didn't want her to have a prepared expectation of it. I didn't want her to go around feeling different. However, *I* wanted to be prepared, so I always knew what I'd say when it happened. I didn't want to stutter and stammer. I wanted her to understand that being called a name doesn't make you what that name signifies. It doesn't define you, but it does define the person saying it to you.

those kids on the bus said. This was the moment it dawned on me that I was different.

I had felt so safe, so accepted; I didn't focus on or really even notice my differences. Even at school, when I got older and a kid would tell a racist joke, they'd preface it by saying, "We can say this in front of you because you don't act black."

Huh?

I wouldn't say anything, but I would think, *What does that mean?* I didn't know what being black meant. My family was the only black family on my street. I was the only black kid in my class, and my brother was the only black kid in his. My mom understood what this meant in a way I couldn't. Despite growing up in an idyllic suburban neighborhood with our perfectly manicured lawns, we weren't immune to racism, Mom knew. And even though I felt I fit in perfectly, I was different.

I wasn't the only person of color in my class—there was Jacob, the Indian kid. But I've been told that I was the first black student to matriculate from kindergarten through twelfth grade in the Chappaqua School District. My mom would tell me that at parent-teacher conferences she could immediately spot my self-portrait because it would be the only one with dark skin.

In second grade, I was heading to assembly with my class when some kids said to me, "Is that your sister?"

They pointed to the third-grade class lined up across the hall from us. In their midst was a little black girl I'd never seen at the school before. *She must be new,* I thought.

"No, that's not my sister. I don't even know her."

But I desperately wanted to know her! A few days later, I was shopping at the A&P, a grocery store in Millwood, with Chris and my mom. There was the girl!

"That's her," I whispered to my mom. "That's the new girl at my school!"

Mom talked to her mom, exchanged phone numbers, and the rest is history—we became inseparable. Toni lived in Chappaqua, which was too far for me to walk or ride my bike from my house, although I did it once and my mom drove me and my bike home. So I was always begging Mom to drive me to her house, or she was begging her mom to drive her to mine. We played for hours and hours. We'd have tea parties and dress up in her mom's elegant clothes. We'd set out to explore the woods behind my house or the wetlands behind hers.

We also played with our matching Sasha dolls, the first brown-skinned doll I owned. Toni had a collection of Sasha dolls, and when I saw them, I knew I had to have one, too. Sasha had big brown eyes and came dressed in a brown corduroy jumper over a white Peter Pan–collared shirt. Unlike most dolls that had stiff, wiry hair, Sasha had long, manageable hair. Toni and I would braid and twist and comb her hair all day long. That doll meant so much to me that when I was choosing names for my youngest daughter, I picked Sasha. And I asked Toni to be her godmother.

When my parents had decided to move out of their Bronx apartment and into a house in Westchester, they circled an area between their teaching jobs—Mom in Ossining and Dad in Elmsford. They settled on New Castle, a hamlet in upper Westchester that comprised Chappaqua and Millwood. Millwood, a working-class suburb, was more affordable. It was a quaint little village with a few shops, a supermarket, a church, and a gas station. Everybody knew everybody else. No one locked their front doors and the kids roamed freely until bells were rung or voices called them in for dinner. Most of the dads worked in town or near town, while the moms stayed home, taking care of the little ones and watching the older ones get on and off the school bus.

On weekends my parents drove around the area finding homes

for sale. One day they stumbled on a three-bedroom raised ranch house. It wasn't exactly what they were looking for—but they couldn't resist the allure of the two-acre property. They put in an offer of $32,000. A week later they found out their offer was accepted.

That's when some of the neighbors began making a stink. One family spread a rumor that my parents couldn't obtain a mortgage. This neighbor even called the seller and pretended to represent the mortgage company. Another homeowner suggested a few residents pool their resources and buy the house to insure no "blacks" moved in. But the seller, who lived across the street and had built his house and our house, wanted my parents to buy it.

Growing up, I didn't know any of this. I played flashlight tag and hide-and-seek with some of the children whose parents didn't want us moving in. My father lent tools and helped repair cars, plumbing, and appliances for some of the neighbors who had originally opposed the idea of him. No one could resist my dad. He became everyone's favorite neighbor and adviser. Sometimes it drove my mother crazy. "Who's he talking to now?" she'd hiss. I think she always felt my dad was being taken advantage of, but he did it all out of the goodness of his heart. As a little girl, I thought he was the smartest guy in the neighborhood.

Besides being the only black family on the street, my mom was one of the few mothers who worked. So she really didn't have much in common with the stay-at-home moms in the neighborhood. She taught music at Claremont, a public elementary school in Ossining, gave private lessons at our house, and played piano and organ for Saint Theresa's, our local parish.

One of my favorite childhood memories is of going to weddings with my mother. I'd sit in Mom's bathroom and study her as she did her makeup before we'd head to church. Mom always applied the same latte-colored foundation. Then she'd dab powder on her face. She wore her lipstick down to this little perfect nub. Then she'd put all her makeup in a small snap bag. Sometimes she'd put her hair back with an Afro puff at the top. When I was little, Mom would wash my hair, then she'd sit me by the stove, take a comb, and put it on the burner to get it hot. She'd coat my hair with Afro Sheen, the hair relaxer, and comb it straight.

I loved watching Mom play at weddings. I'd sit on the bench next to her and turn the pages of her sheet music while she played traditional wedding songs on the organ. I realized that a wedding was about many things—the flowers, the gowns, the kiss, the couple, love—but Mom's music brought it to life.

My parents wanted me to love music and dance as much as they did. So while I was in nursery school my mother enrolled me in beginner ballet classes at the community center. I wore a pink leotard and matching tights as I learned the five positions. After a few classes, the instructor told my mother that I was really talented and suggested I take more challenging classes. Mom enrolled me at the Steffi Nossen School of Dance (where I continued studying through high school). I can still remember my mother beaming as she watched me through the glass partitions. I was so happy to know she was looking at me. I wanted to be as talented as my mother. I was in awe of my mother's talents. I was in awe of my mother.

But I really didn't know who she was.

*The family that plays together, stays together.*

*Our family home in Millwood, New York*

*Maura, me, and Toni*

ROARING
BROOK
SCHOOL
CHAPPAQUA
1971
GRADE -2

*Miss Boley's second-grade class*

# CHAPTER

## 7

I was an eight-year-old girl in a heavy brown coat, holding my sisters' hands tightly as we were forced to say the words that changed our world.

We stood in front of a stern-looking judge who presided over adoption court.

"Who do you want to live with?" he asked Sandra, Gretta, and me.

"Our grandparents," we whispered, even though the thought terrified us.

We wanted to stay with our mother and baby brother, Sonny. Our grandparents were abusive people. (I found out years later that they could not have been our biological grandparents. I heard my grandmother say that she had had an accident and couldn't ever have children. They must have adopted my dad. I believe his biological parents were biracial—that's why Vanessa and Chris have blue eyes. Milton and I have the recessive trait.)

I learned how to hold back tears at a young age. Even now, I rarely cry in public. Usually it's when I'm all alone—in the shower or the bathtub. Then I let it all out.

We lived with my "grandparents" on the second floor of a two-family house in Buffalo and were told to call them "Momma" and "Daddy." I didn't know where my father lived. He worked for the railroads and made trips to Buffalo from time to time. But I knew exactly where my mother lived—in a house two blocks away.

I wasn't allowed to visit her, see her, or talk to her. We never asked why. We understood that it was better not to ask.

All I knew is that my mother worked as a domestic. One day I was standing on the corner near my house. I saw my mother on the bus that the maids took to and from work. She looked right at me. I stared at her but didn't acknowledge her. I didn't wave. I didn't even smile. I knew I'd get in trouble. I was terrified that someone was watching. Someone always seemed to be watching. I never said anything about it to anyone, not even my sisters.

Each year at Christmastime, a taxi drove to our house and dropped off presents from my mother—books and toys. I was allowed to call her to say thank you. I still remember the phone number—Cleveland 4880. My grandparents hovered over me as I spoke to her. I didn't say anything more than thank you. I was afraid to speak.

My grandparents were always angry with us. Almost every day I got some kind of beating. I was hit with belts, leather straps, and rough, strong hands. Most times I'd have no idea what I did wrong. One day I was washing dishes and "Daddy" noticed I didn't clean the bottom of the pot. He hit me with a leather strap for that. Another time I questioned something I had to do—what, I'm not sure. "Momma" took a nasal inhaler and shoved it up my nose while holding my other nostril closed with her fingers. I struggled to breathe.

I felt myself getting dizzy and about to lose consciousness. She finally let go.

"Daddy" worked at Bethlehem Steel. My sisters and I would get up at three or four in the morning and sit in a chair in the living room while he got ready for work. I don't know why we had to do this. Again, something we dared not question. We'd sit there watching him, struggling to keep our sleepy eyes open. When he left, we'd get ready for school.

My real father would visit every now and then. He was charming, handsome, and a really good dancer. He'd tell me he was a hoofer. I remember going out for dinner and watching him flirt with the waitresses. When he'd visit, my father would ask me to sing *"O Mio Babbino Caro"* ("Oh, My Beloved Father") from the opera *Gianni Schicchi* by Giacomo Puccini. It was his favorite piece of music and it became one of my favorites, too.

My father would breeze in and out of town. He'd stay for a short time and then before we'd know it, he'd just disappear. We had no idea where he went.

From the outside we seemed like a happy family. No one would suspect what was really going on behind the doors of 198 Hickory Street. I wore nice, stylish clothes. I was well-groomed. I went to school on time every day.

The one kind thing my grandparents did was to sign me up for piano lessons. It saved me. I found my escape in music. I would lose myself at the tiny spinet in the living room. I played viola and sang in the choir, too. My sisters and I performed as the Tinch Sisters at black churches all around the city. I played piano and sang songs—mostly spiritual music, such as "There's a Balm in Gilead" and "Oh! What a Beautiful City," which are still two of my favorite songs. I don't know if we got paid. It was just something we did. We didn't question it.

I studied so hard and so much that I always got high honors. I skipped seventh grade. School and music were my lifeline to sanity. At that time most black students went on to a technical high school, but a teacher saw my potential and encouraged me to go to Buffalo's East High School, which had a real curriculum and offered me a real future. I'd never considered college because no one in my family had gone, but my teachers there showed me that it was possible.

I entered State University of Fredonia on a scholarship when I was sixteen. I majored in music education. I was so happy to get away. I finally felt free.

One day I realized I didn't have to follow my grandparents' orders anymore. I started writing to my mother from college. I misspelled her last name on the envelope for years, always writing Doris Griffen when I should have written Griffin. She never corrected my mistake. I guess she was just happy to hear from me.

Years later, Milton, Vanessa, Chris, and I would make the eight-hour drive to visit my mother. We'd park in the back of the project where she lived behind a chain-link fence on Jefferson Street. Before we'd walk into the courtyard, we'd see her perched up in her kitchen window in apartment F, smiling down at us. She'd lived in the same apartment most of her adult life, so everyone knew her. She was the queen bee of the neighborhood until she died of complications from diabetes at the age of sixty-five.

Her headstone at Forest Lawn Cemetery in Buffalo reads: GRANDMOTHER OF THE FIRST BLACK MISS AMERICA.

She never did tell me why we lived two blocks away from her and had to pretend we didn't know her.

Then again, I never asked.

*"What a Difference a Day Makes"*
My mother, Doris Griffin, December 8
(my birthday)

*"Midnight Train to Georgia"*
My father, Edward Tinch

*"I Will Survive"*
World, here I come!

*"Let the Good Times Roll"*
*The Tinch sisters: Gretta, Sandra, and Helen*

# CHAPTER 8

*Vanessa had her secrets—I understood that. All children keep things from their parents. But there were times when she was an adolescent that I felt I didn't know her at all.*

—HELEN WILLIAMS

When I was ten, family friends who had a daughter two years older invited me to visit their friends in Orange County, California. I figured my strict parents would never allow me to go away with Nancy and her parents. But Mom and Dad were busy traveling back and forth to the hospital to visit Uncle Artie, my dad's younger brother. He was really sick with cirrhosis and the prognosis wasn't very good. I suppose they figured they'd let me get away for a week and have an adventure. I was shocked but so excited. I'd never been on a trip without my parents.

Their home was about an hour south of Los Angeles and crammed with row after row of identical white stucco tract houses. The flat, dry land was filled with housing developments as well as construction sites for future developments. Thinking back on it now, it looked like the setting for a movie like *E.T.* or *Poltergeist*. It wasn't exactly the California I had imagined.

The family we stayed with had two kids—Susan, who was eighteen, and John, who was twelve. Susan smoked, drove a car, and was the epitome of cool—at least to my ten-year-old brain. I always wanted to hang out with older kids. I couldn't wait to be older, to be independent, and Susan treated us like we were older kids. She drove us to all the tourist destinations—Disneyland, Hollywood, the beach. She'd let us sneak a puff of her cigarette.

John was close to my age. As soon as I met him, I had a little crush on him. We all spent a lot of time playing outside when we weren't sightseeing. One evening John and I wandered over to a construction site filled with big concrete pipes stacked on top of one another. We sat on a pipe and talked about school and friends.

Then John leaned in and kissed me. He had braces and they banged against my lips. It was a quick peck and then it was over. But it was thrilling for me—it felt like a big moment in my life. I had finally kissed a boy. We walked back to the house and I smiled the whole way.

Nancy and I slept in the den on two sofa beds. We whispered and giggled about my moment with John. I finally drifted off to sleep, dreaming of my kiss.

I don't know how long I was asleep—minutes? Hours? But at some point, the accordion door to the den slowly opened and Susan crept in. I couldn't figure out why she was in our room in the middle of the night.

Susan whispered, "Be quiet."

She told me to get out of bed and lie down on the rug.

I was confused. I looked over at Nancy, who was sleeping soundly. Are we going to play a game? As I tried to make sense of why this older girl wanted me to lie on the rug, Susan pulled down the yellow bloomers of my cotton baby-doll pajamas.

"What are you doing?" I asked.

"Don't worry—it'll feel good." I lay there paralyzed as she moved her tongue between my legs. What was going on? I didn't speak. She kept at this for I don't know how long. But it felt good, weird, and definitely wrong—all at the same time. She slid my bloomers back up and whispered: "Don't tell anyone."

I watched her as she crept back out. I climbed into my bed, still tingling at ten years old, trying to figure out what had just happened. Why had she done that? Was it something teenagers did to each other? Only girls? I thought it had to be something bad—why would she have told me not to tell anyone?

I woke up the next morning feeling confused. We were heading back to New York and I couldn't wait to get out of that house and away from Susan. Then on the flight home, I thought about it some more. I just wanted to get home and see my parents. I couldn't tell my mom about this because it felt naughty. I imagined her looking at me hard and saying, "Oh, Vanessa, what were you thinking? Why didn't you say no?"

But maybe I'd be able to talk to my dad.

When I got off the plane and saw my parents waiting at the top of the Jetway, I knew something terrible had happened while I was away. My father had lost weight and his skin was ashen. He looked so, so sad.

"Uncle Artie died," Mom said.

My confusion and fears were evaporated by my family's grief. I pushed Susan's late-night visit to the back of my mind as we mourned for Uncle Artie. Dad was devastated by his brother's death—Uncle Artie had been a really talented basketball player, but he had a heart murmur and couldn't pursue his dream of playing professionally. He just kind of drank himself to death. My father took it really hard and never recovered from this loss.

And that's how the summer ended—with a funeral and burial. Then it was back to school. I tried to forget about Susan. When I couldn't, I struggled to make sense of it. I thought, *Okay, there's this thing I did—it felt good, and since it was with another girl, it was probably okay.* That's how I rationalized it. But even as I told myself this, I felt it wasn't really okay at all.

For years I kept Susan's visit to myself. Most girls remember their first kiss fondly, but every time I thought about sitting on the pipes at the construction site with John, I'd get this yucky feeling. My thoughts would always be overshadowed by Susan with her dark purple bedroom and the way she pretended to be the cool older kid to a ten-year-old on a summer vacation. Even today, if I see a dark purple room, it just brings me back to that trip and I get a weird, sickening feeling in my gut.

I didn't really understand what had happened until I was in college. I was with my boyfriend, Bruce, and it just hit me and I blurted it out: "Oh my God—I was molested!"

It took me almost a decade to realize that I was an innocent victim and Susan was an eighteen-year-old predator. She had manipulated me the entire trip, just so that she could take advantage of me and I wouldn't speak a word of it.

Years later, when I was suing *Penthouse* for printing the photos of me with another woman, my lawyers told me that Bob Guccione's attorneys would grill me on any sexual relationships I'd ever had with men . . . and women. My mind immediately went back to my trip to California. I thought I'd probably have to tell them about Susan. I imagined the headlines.

After that trip, I felt something change in me. I had always been defiant, but I became a bit more rebellious. I began to pull away from my parents, which devastated my dad. We'd been so close. I always felt I could tell him anything—and then I just kept to myself.

My parents blamed it on approaching adolescence and hormones. But I wonder if part of me was acting out the anger and confusion I felt over Susan's late-night visit.

# CHAPTER 9

*I think my children felt very loved when they were little. But when they turned into adolescents, when it really mattered because they felt uncomfortable in their skin, I had a hard time showing them affection. I wish I could do it over again and show them my love at a time they really needed it.*

—HELEN WILLIAMS

My fourth grade teacher, Mr. Hart, gave everyone a nickname; mine was "Van Can." He'd chime, "Van Can do it all—winter, spring, summer, fall." That year, he decided we'd produce a play based on our Greek mythology studies. He gave students various assignments—writing, acting, costuming. He knew I was a dancer, so he asked me, "Van Can," to choreograph a dance that would be my solo.

Westorchard Elementary School in Chappaqua was a very progressive school for its time. The classrooms had partitions, which could be rolled back to allow another grade to join discussions. Sometimes third and fourth grade would be combined. The teachers also tried to make learning as creative as possible. Mr. Hart, a tall, lanky, dynamic man, was just one of the many excellent teachers I had.

I loved school. I loved my teachers. I loved learning. It was such an encouraging and very safe environment.

For *The Trojan Horse*, a group of us wrote a song, created our costumes, and played recorders to accompany the music. I can still remember some of the lyrics: "Where are thou, men of Greece, return home soon, remove our gloom."

I'd done a lot of recitals—dance and piano—but this was my first role in a school play with an audience. I was a natural and performing made me joyous. If there was a play, I'd be in it. Even at home, Chris and I and our cousins or the neighbors would set up a stage in front of the fireplace and sing, dance, and act for my parents, neighbors, aunts, uncles—whoever was over for dinner. "Let's put on a show" was something you were sure to hear if you were a dinner guest at the Williamses' house.

When I wasn't performing, I enjoyed watching other performers. I loved the glamour of the old Technicolor movies with big musical numbers and glittery costumes. I was hooked and could watch them for hours on weekends. Fred Astaire, Ginger Rogers, Rita Hayworth, and Gene Kelly were some of my favorites. Some of my all-time favorite movies were *Kiss Me Kate*, *Singin' in the Rain*, anything with Danny Kaye, *Cinderfella* with Jerry Lewis, Rodgers and Hammerstein's *Cinderella*, and, of course, *The Wizard of Oz*, which was a treat once a year.

You could see all the choreography and watch performers from head to toe. There weren't close-ups of someone's face or feet to make you wonder if it was really them. In these old movies, you knew the actors had to do it all—there were no doubles performing the tough moves. They were all triple threats.

Mom fueled my interest by taking me into the city to see almost every hot black show on Broadway—*Your Arms Too Short to Box with*

*God, Eubie!*, and *Purlie*, to name a few. But when I saw *The Wiz*, I was mesmerized. I wanted to be Stephanie Mills. She sang, she danced, she acted. She did it all and she was great at all of it—plus she was close to my age. She made Broadway seem attainable. I wanted to do this someday.

The stage was alluring to me. For as long as I could remember, I wanted to be a performer. (Except for that time when I was about six and I thought that being a stewardess was the most glamorous job in the world. It was the seventies—what can I say!) I thought I'd be a Rockette at Radio City Music Hall. Or a singer. Or a performer on a variety show. Or a dancer with a prestigious company like Alvin Ailey.

Then I saw Stephanie Mills and I knew. I wanted to be on Broadway.

*Van Can do it all.*

My dad never pushed performing on me. His attitude was "Whatever she likes, well, that's fine with me. I just want her to have a happy life."

My mother made a point of subtly showing me that I shouldn't ever put limits on myself. If we went to Radio City to watch the Rockettes, she'd say something like, "Those Rockettes do a great job. Wouldn't it be interesting to be the first black Rockette?" Or if we were at a play watching the orchestra, she'd point out a black instrumentalist. "Look at that black girl on the French horn. Isn't she wonderful? Wouldn't that be a great career?" (I ended up playing French horn for nine years.)

Mom was constantly putting it in my head that I could break the mold, I could be different. "Dare to be different" was a poster on a wall in our home. I suppose part of it was because she was always singled out; she was always breaking obstacles when she was young. She never told me what I should do, but she made me aware that just because I didn't see someone who looked like me on the stage or in the orchestra, it didn't mean that the goal was out of my reach. It just hadn't been done yet. And why couldn't I be the one to do it?

My parents told me that they could pinpoint the moment when they saw that spark of something special in me. It was seventh grade, and I was part of the ensemble cast of the Robert E. Bell Middle School production of the musical *Little Mary Sunshine*. I don't remember much about it, other than I had a solo dance. To what? I'm not sure. Mom said that halfway through the performance, she and my dad just looked at each other. *WOW!* It was a look that said "Vanessa's got it."

It was a moment my parents realized I could do something with this natural ability to sing, dance, and act. They said I had a small part but I seemed larger than life. They'd seen me in a few productions, but this was different. Mom said when I was onstage, the audience focused on me as if there was no one else. The local newspaper ran a photo of me—my first newspaper clipping.

"Good job, Ness," my mom said. If Mom paid me a compliment, I knew I had been fantastic.

I started sixth grade as a straight-A student and, for the most part, a pretty obedient daughter. (Well, with some lapses.) But by the time I had spent my three years at Bell Middle School, I had changed. I was annoyed with my parents the majority of the time. (What adolescent isn't?) I tried to shut my parents out and had a big case of selective hearing.

My mother was the target for most of my moods. I'd be snippy, impatient, or plain sassy at times. I'd roll my eyes and talk back or just walk out of the room while she was speaking. And watch out! You don't do that to my mother!

"Go to your room and come out when I tell you to," she'd yell at me nearly every day. She'd squeeze my arm and that meant business.

Mom took my mood swings personally, but I was raging with

hormones and couldn't help myself. Mom didn't know how to handle this force that I had become—lamb in sixth grade, lion in seventh. As a teacher, she taught elementary school students. She'd say, "I hate middle school kids. I just can't stand that age." I think even before I got there, she had convinced herself that it would be pure hell.

The family times I had cherished—reading with Dad, playing Operation or Connect Four with Chris, and family badminton matches—started to seem silly to me. Hanging out with my friends was a priority.

Mom would give me her icy stare. "What's the matter with you? What's happened to you? Who are you?"

Now that I have children, I understand this age better—all children break away from their parents—but back then, I didn't know what was going on. When my oldest daughter, Melanie, became an adolescent and started the moody and irritable part, I took it personally at first. I even made the other kids promise they wouldn't act like that. But I learned that a lot of it just can't be helped. They don't even realize they're doing it. With each child, I learned to be more aware and compassionate and less reactive.

And Mom, maybe because of the way she was raised, seemed completely perplexed. Sure, I knew I was changing—I was developing breasts and beginning my battle with acne. Dad seemed to understand that I was growing up and needed some space of my own, but Mom was annoyed and frustrated. Dad would often find himself stuck in the middle, trying to make peace. But how do you subdue two hurricanes?

My mother will say that my dad was the leader of the household, but I didn't see it that way at all. They worked together. They always seemed to be in agreement. But my dad was always more approachable. I hate to use the word "soft" because that implies weakness, and he wasn't weak at all. He was a strong man who happened to be sensitive to everyone's feelings.

My parents were always a team. There seemed to be a wall between my parents and me. I tell my kids everything—I try to be
their friend—but my parents drew the line. They were such a unit,
and I think that fueled my rebellious streak. They would call me
into the living room for a family meeting. I'd roll my eyes and be
like, "Ugh, do I have to?" I'd sort of just drag myself in there. But I
wouldn't listen. I'd be off thinking about something else (mostly
boys) as they'd outline their grievances with me:

I wasn't coming home when I was supposed to. I was talking
back. I wasn't picking up after myself, and my room was a mess.

My dad would rely on his psychology books to understand me.
He'd try to figure out why I was acting out. He'd explain to me the
cause and effect and the consequences of my actions. Besides being
a music teacher, he was also the vice principal and the disciplinarian
at his school. He'd approach me with the same patience and understanding he gave his students.

My dad was so patient, but my mom was just exasperated with
me. She didn't want to talk about it and analyze it; she wanted to
take action and stop it! One time she stormed into my room, took
everything she could pick up, and just dumped it in the middle of
the floor. "Now, clean it up."

I was furious with her. I had to spend the whole day cleaning my
room.

I think my mom was annoyed that I was growing up. Even when
I was just eleven, my changing body seemed like an inconvenience
to her. I remember going into the bathroom and discovering that I
was bleeding. My period! I called my mother into the bathroom and
excitedly told her, "I got my period!"

"Congratulations. You're a woman now," Mom said.

Okay, that might seem like a normal maternal way to react, but
you had to be there. She said it so matter-of-factly and then let out a
heavy sigh. It was almost resentful. It was like, "Now look what

you've done." There was no hugging, no excitement, just exasperation. My getting my period seemed like a major inconvenience to my mother. Why? Did she think I'd become more hormonal, more difficult, more moody? I wasn't sure.

Now that I'm a mother, I understand better. I was young but I was developing early. So Mom knew I'd be getting attention from older boys who thought I was more mature than I was. She knew I was too young to understand or handle this.

I think my mom was scared.

## HELEN ON PUBERTY

Scared?

Of course I was scared! I thought, "Oh God, here's one more thing to think about with this kid! Let's hope she doesn't get pregnant." Because I never knew what was next with her. I swear I was six feet before I had Vanessa—now I'm barely five one.

I was this force with hormones! "Sit with your knees together," Mom would bark at me. She was always in a state of being on guard, being alert, being protective.

Mom's exasperation is exactly what I channeled into *Ugly Betty*. Wilhelmina, my character, was always annoyed by everyone's inadequacies. Her attitude was, "Get it together, people! UGH! Do I have to do everything?"

That's exactly my mother.

YOU HAVE NO IDEA

*You're a woman now. How could you do this to me? Get it together! And don't get pregnant!*

At Horace Greeley High School in Chappaqua, I immersed myself in performing. I played French horn in the marching band, acted in all the theater productions, and sang in the chorus. I performed in two shows a year and choreographed pieces for the school spring finale with the theater department. Greeley was also a very progressive school and students were able to pick their courses and schedule. We were offered a lot of electives, and most of my time was spent in the performing arts building, studying band, orchestra, voice, and theater.

Like most high schools in Westchester in the late seventies and early eighties, Greeley was divided into the typical cliques. There were the stoners who wore flannel shirts and ripped jeans; the greasers who wore black leather jackets; the rich kids in their Izods who played tennis, skied, and drove BMWs; and the theater kids, who had their own style. If you were a theater kid, you could be different and be cool. I didn't conform to the standard preppy outfit of the time. I would wear my gauchos or knickers with bright-striped socks.

Unlike other schools, the theater department at Greeley had a full-time faculty, and you could take four years' worth of classes in scene study, improv, method acting, and so on. The theater building became my second home. Many people who were active in the theater department when I was there went on to have big Hollywood careers. My friend Adam Belanoff, a writer for *The Closer,* also co–executive produced *The Cosby Show* and *Murphy Brown.* Joe Berlinger became an award-winning documentary film director. Dan Bucatinsky is a television producer (I did the genealogy quest series *Who Do You Think You Are?* with him). Matt Arkin, the son of actor Alan Arkin, directed me in my freshman spring finale.

As a sophomore, I got my first big break when I landed the lead in the Madwoman of Chaillot musical *Dear World*. My photo appeared in the local paper. More clippings for the scrapbook. I was becoming a hometown star. "Great job," Mom said. And again, when my mom says something like this, I know she's impressed!

During the summers, I performed in various productions—*Once Upon a Mattress, The Two Gentlemen of Verona, Of Thee I Sing*—for the Saw Mill Summer Theatre, Chappaqua's community theater for performers from fourteen to twenty-four. I also choreographed *The Robber Bridegroom* one year. Plus, I always had a job.

I was doing it all—marching at football games, starring in shows, traveling with our orchestra, dancing in recitals. Between school, work, theater, and dance, I didn't have any time to get in trouble.

Well . . .

Unfortunately I could find the time for trouble—or it found me. It seemed with each year, I became more and more rebellious. The girl who rode her bike without considering the crash grew into the girl who tried to sneak out at night, who ignored curfews, who smoked pot. The girl still loved the thrill of adventure, except as I got older, the risks became greater—and the consequences bigger.

My mom and dad tried to keep me in check. My dad would ask me to write up contracts promising to be good, which he'd put on the refrigerator. My mom still has these promissory notes I'd written as a teenager.

*"I, Vanessa Williams, promise to abide to the rules of the Williamses' house as long as I am residing here. I will not allow anyone in the house to use the telephone without permission. I will not do anything illegal or otherwise, and I wouldn't do anything considered wrong, and if not sure, I would ask."*

Let's just say if it was wrong, I never asked. What's the point in asking when you know the answer is NO?

When I grew out of my little-girl pale pink room, Dad and I turned my bedroom into an autumnal forest. We had hung up a big mural of woods, with trees with gold, orange, and rust-colored leaves. I had gold shag carpeting and a lime green bedspread that matched my walls. The northeast light flooded my room in the morning and my windows looked out on the street, so I could see who was coming and going.

It was important for me to love my room because I spent most of my adolescent years stuck in it, stripped of privileges for more reasons than I can remember. Sometimes Chris would tell on me; he was four years younger, so he was being what younger brothers are . . . intrusive.

I was grounded all the time. There was always a different circumstance, a different group of kids, a different story. My mother would catch me at something and I'd be grounded again. Then I'd sneak out some more. It was this endless circle. It seemed I was always slamming my door in anger.

One day, after too many door slammings, Dad calmly came to my room with a screwdriver, took the door off its hinges, and stored it in the garage.

"If you don't respect the rules of the house, you don't get a door," he said. "You don't deserve privacy."

The door was off my bedroom for months.

In high school, I played the mellophone, an instrument similar to the French horn but shaped like a trumpet and with a bigger bell, for the school's marching band. There were three parts of the band—the musicians, the cheerleaders, and the silks. Sometimes after school and before practice, a bunch of us would smoke pot to make rehearsals more fun. We weren't burnouts, we weren't even stoners. It was just something that we'd do once in a while to get silly and laugh. It was more of a bonding thing. Of course I rarely got away with anything. When I came home after practice one day, my mom was waiting for me at the top of the stairs.

My eyes were bloodshot. *So what was my excuse? Let me think!*

Mom looked at me and I could tell she knew I was high. "I must be allergic to my mascara."

It turned out my mom and dad had found a small bag of pot in a tiny compartment in the secretary in my bedroom.

"Get in the car. We're going to school," they said.

I tried to explain that I wasn't some pothead with stashes of marijuana. Did they think I was dealing drugs and smoking all the time? When we got to school, they made me take them to my locker so they could inspect it—in front of the other kids! It was so embarrassing to have my parents standing next to me as I opened my locker and pulled everything out. I think Mom expected to find it packed with pot, but there was nothing there.

"See, I told you," I said. But they weren't convinced that I didn't have a problem.

Another time, during a sleepover at my house, my friend and I were watching late-night television and we smoked a bowl in the greenhouse. When we were finished I dumped the remainder in some dirt and went back into the house to watch TV.

A few months later, my mom went on a tirade.

"How dare you, Ness! How dare you!"

"What now?" I had no idea what my mother was screaming about.

"You planted pot in the greenhouse! What were you thinking?"

I looked at her like she was crazy. "Are you kidding me? I'm not growing pot in the greenhouse!"

"Are you going to deny this to my face?" Mom hissed. "Then you really are a great actress."

"I swear I did not do this."

Years later I realized what had happened—the seeds from the pot must have taken root and sprouted. But to this day, if I bring it up with my mother, she will say I was growing pot in our house! I'm not that stupid!

But the family meetings and disappointment continued. "There are certain things we don't do as a family. These are the rules. We don't come in late. We don't treat people with disrespect," Dad or Mom would say. When it came to marijuana, they'd say, "Do you realize what you're doing to your body? Your brain? And what happens when you get bored of marijuana? This could lead to something else—something more powerful and more dangerous. We don't do that in our family."

My parents never said, "You're bad." There was never any name-calling. Instead, it was always very inclusive. "We are a family," they would say. "These are the things we as a family don't do. You're part of the family, so we expect you to abide by our rules."

Unlike elementary school, where I was one of the only black kids, in high school there was a group of us black girls who hung out together during free time. We even had our own cafeteria table where we'd meet at lunch, talk, and make plans for the weekend.

During my sixteenth summer, I went to a party at my friend Lori's house in Chappaqua. While we were dancing in her garage, a car full of black guys just happened to drive by. Black guys in Chappaqua? I suppose they were equally surprised to see a bunch of black girls dancing in a garage in Chappaqua.

Joe got out and introduced himself. He was twenty years old and a gorgeous bodybuilder with the whitest teeth and the biggest smile I'd ever seen. He was the oldest of nine kids who lived in Katonah, a nearby town. He had dreams of playing football but was studying to be a mortician—yes, a mortician—at Westchester Community College.

He asked for my phone number. He called the next day and asked for a date. When my mom met him, she liked him right away. I knew she thought he was very good-looking, and he actually thought my mom was hot. Yuck! You don't want to hear that coming from your boyfriend!

Joe was one of those guys who was striking and really polite. He'd do and say all the right things—he'd shake my father's and mother's hand, smile at them, and promise to have me home on time—and he always did. But in between pick-up and curfew, he'd get busy with me in his station wagon. When he'd drop me off later, he'd again be the perfect gentleman in front of my parents. It was all a very well-polished act.

To Mom, Joe was this really good guy from a nice Catholic family. He was respectful. He was well-mannered. He was the perfect boyfriend.

## HELEN ON JOE

Oh, please! He was the perfect boyfriend because I knew it wasn't serious. It wasn't going to last. But boy, was he good-looking. They made a striking couple.

And then there was Bruce. . . .

I met Bruce while I was at a New Year's Eve party with Joe. We had been together a year and we were bored. Joe was gorgeous, athletic, nice as can be, but there wasn't much of a challenge. My mother will say I get bored too easily.

So while we went to the party as a couple, I was in the living room counting down to midnight and dancing to the music, and Joe was upstairs flirting with a buxom girl with long black hair, who happened to be Pam Grier's cousin. When midnight struck, I embraced my friend Toni, and this handsome sandy-brown-haired guy with deep-set brown eyes came up to me.

"Happy New Year," he said. And then he kissed me on the lips. WHEW!

"Happy New Year to you," I said. Then he just walked away.

*Okay, who is this guy who just walks up to me and kisses me on the lips?* I was shocked by his boldness, especially since he knew that I was with my bodybuilder boyfriend who was right upstairs.

Wait, what bodybuilder boyfriend again? (Maybe Mom was right about my attention span.)

I ended it with Joe shortly thereafter and began dating Bruce. We fell in love very quickly. He was a freshman at Fairleigh Dickinson University. He was this really smart, sophisticated, and well-traveled guy, who had a lot of black friends. Bruce's best friend, Gary, was black and dating my best friend, Toni. He was used to being around black people and he loved black music. In his free time, Bruce skied, played tennis, and rode horses. He worked at a cocktail bar in Saratoga, so he knew how to mix proper drinks. He knew how to cook. He was a really well-rounded guy. His parents—his mom was a teacher, his father owned a car dealership—had just gotten divorced, so I'm sure I was an escape from all that stress for him.

My parents couldn't stand us together. I was impulsive and Bruce was ready for anything, which was a dangerous combination. My mom felt that I had this bright future, but I was willing to risk everything for Bruce. My mom would say, "What are we going to do with you?" They couldn't control me. There was no punishment that mattered to me. Every time I was grounded, I'd sneak out anyway. I was ready to take the heat. I'd disobey them. But I didn't care. Bruce always let me have my way, which infuriated my parents. They felt he didn't respect their rules.

It was crazy young love. I'd lie about where I'd been, but Mom always knew. I'd be out with Bruce, miss curfew, and make no apologies. My parents would be waiting up. Then I'd get the lecture.

In high school, Mom always found scholarships for me. During my senior year, she had applied for a scholarship for me through the National Foundation for Advancement in the Arts. As a finalist, I was invited to a weekend drama program at Princeton University, where I performed monologues from Molière's *The Misanthrope* and Ntozake Shange's 1975 stage play *For Colored Girls Who Have Considered Suicide When the Rainbow Is Enuf.*

Bruce met me there. We couldn't stand to be apart.

Mom found out.

When I returned from Princeton, I was in my room, kneeling on the floor, unpacking my suitcase. No one else was home but Mom and me. Mom stormed in and yanked me by the hair and forced me up off the floor.

"You're ruining your life. You're not going to graduate," she screamed. What was she talking about? Of course I'd graduate!

I tried to stay calm. She's so tiny next to me—just over five feet. So I walked out of the room. But that infuriated her, so she followed me. I kept moving. She followed. She chased me around the living room coffee table and then back into my room. Mom had become this other person I didn't know—she was consumed with rage and fear. She got right in my face and grabbed me. I pushed her off me. She stumbled into a lamp that hit the wall and landed on the floor.

Getting physical was not something that we did in our family. My dad spanked me once and then never again. This time was different. What was going on?

When Dad and Chris returned home, we didn't say a word.

Mom was disgusted that her anger had reached the boiling point. She was also very, very sad. I think she felt she'd lost me.

My father was just as upset with me, but he would keep it inside, trying to understand, trying to be patient. I'm sure he'd headed to his psychology books and struggled to figure me out.

But the anger was bubbling in him as well. And then one day it just exploded.

Bruce and I had been apart since I had traveled to the Bahamas on an orchestra trip. We needed to see each other—desperately. The plan was to fake going to school. I pretended to wait for my ride on another street. Bruce parked his maroon Camaro on the next street over. I waited until the house was empty and then headed back inside. Mom and Dad were teaching all day, and Chris was at school—no one would be home for hours.

I made breakfast. Then we headed downstairs to the pullout sofa in Dad's den and turned on the stereo full blast. We started kissing, undressing, making love, and then . . .

The music went off.

*Uh oh.*

If the music clicked off, that could only mean one thing!

"VANESSA!"

Mom was standing over us, horrified.

*Performing "Love Me" as Silvia in* THE TWO GENTLEMEN OF VERONA *at Saw Mill Summer Theatre, 1979*

*My first lead as the Madwoman of Chaillot in* DEAR WORLD *at Horace Greeley High School*

*Mother Hare in* THE GOLDEN APPLE, *Syracuse University*

*Posing in the Robert E. Bell Middle School gym doors
with Gail, Christy, and Liz*

I left school to deposit money in the bank at lunchtime. Then I decided to do something I never do—eat lunch at home. As I approached my home, I saw what I thought was Bruce's car down the street, but it just never dawned on me that he'd be in the house. It was a weekday—Vanessa was supposed to be at school!

I walked into the house and was greeted by the smell of bacon and the sound of blasting music. I was completely baffled for a moment.

Who cooked bacon and why was there music on?

And then it hit me.

Vanessa!

Why would Vanessa be home when she should be at school?

Bruce!

What were they doing here?

OH MY GOD!

I stormed downstairs to the stereo and switched it off. Then I tried to gain some composure as I headed into the den.

There they were. On *my* pullout sofa.

AGHHHH!

I don't know what I said, if I said anything. I stood there completely horrified as they quickly covered themselves up.

I was furious. I can't remember when I ever felt that angry before or since. I was enraged and I was scared of what I'd do. I just knew I had to take a step back. I was afraid that I might hurt somebody if I stayed in that room.

I slowly walked out and tried to control myself from doing bodily damage to somebody because I was so upset, so frustrated.

I picked up the phone and very calmly spoke to Milton.

"I'm here at the house with Vanessa and Bruce. I think you should come home."

That's all I said. That's all I had to say. Milton understood.

Normally it took about twenty minutes for Milton to get home from his school, but he was there in ten. He walked in the house and he was furious. And to make matters worse, Vanessa and Bruce were sitting together, all cuddly, in the same small chair. I think they were even holding hands. They weren't at all embarrassed. They didn't apologize. Their attitude was "Oh, we got caught—what's the big deal?"

And this just made Milton even more furious.

He walked up to Bruce and punched him in the face.

WHAT?

Who is this person?

You have to understand my husband. He's the calmest person I've ever known. I'd been married to him for twenty years then, and I'd never seen him like this. He never hit anyone. It's just not in his nature. If he was angry, he believed in talking it out, not hitting. But I'd never seen him angry like this before.

This was about so much more than just walking in on Bruce and Vanessa. Although what parent ever wants to see that? This was about months and months of being treated with disrespect by them. This was about months and months of being ignored. Bruce didn't respect us as Vanessa's parents. He'd use any chance he could to show us that he had a certain amount of influence over Vanessa that we no longer had. He seemed to enjoy making us aware of this.

And to make matters worse, even though I'd walked in on them like that, they didn't seem to care. If they had acted a little bit sorry for what they did, I feel like Milton would have been upset but not so furious. But Bruce sat there as if nothing was wrong. Milton wanted both of them to understand that something was *very* wrong. For the first time in his life, Milton knew that he couldn't get through to them with words.

Bruce's lip was bleeding. We told him to leave the house.

A few minutes later, a policeman came to the door. He'd seen Bruce out front with a bloody lip and wanted to make sure everything was okay.

"Everything's fine," I said, trying to sound as calm as possible—even though nothing was fine at all.

Milton went back to work.

I drove Vanessa to school.

I didn't speak. What could I say? There were no words she'd listen to, no punishment she'd take seriously.

We felt lost. We felt like we were in the middle of a crisis. Vanessa seemed gone to us. We had no idea what to do or where to go from here.

It was a hard, hard time.

*A hard, hard time.*

# PART THREE

# THE
# SWEETEST DAYS

# CHAPTER 11

I was sixteen and a freshman at State University of New York at Fredonia when I heard the rumors of a cute, popular, black senior. Then one day, as I was walking to music class with a friend, I spotted him. It wasn't too difficult—there weren't that many black students at Fredonia.

My version is that I saw him and thought, *Hmmm, he's cute.* Milton's version is that I saw him and excitedly exclaimed: "That's him! That's him!"

Now does that really sound like me? I'm much more subtle. Milton was very handsome—he was tall, with the most beautiful smile. Okay, he might have caught me staring a bit. Our eyes met and we continued along our separate ways.

Our friends thought we'd be perfect for each other, so they arranged for us to meet in the school snack bar, where Milton worked. He asked me to the movies and I said yes.

I don't remember what movie we saw, but I do remember the bats in the balcony that kept flying in front of the screen. Afterward, I thought, *He's interesting.* He was this very accomplished musician who could really play the tenor saxophone. We had a lot in common. We were the first members of our families to go to college. We also were music education majors. We wanted to go on to graduate school and then teach music.

But where I felt unloved and mistreated, Milton was the golden boy of a family that was just full of love and affection for one another. Milton Augustine Jr. was named for his father and was the middle child of five kids—three boys and two girls. His family called him Billy, and in their eyes, he was perfect.

We had another thing in common—neither of us knew our mothers. His mom was twenty-eight years old when she died of pre-eclampsia and a heart attack shortly after giving birth to her fifth child, Arthur, who weighed a watermelon-size 13.5 pounds. Milton was only three and didn't have many memories of her. Years later, my son, Chris, told a story about asking his dad what he remembered about his mother. After a long pause, Milton smiled wistfully. "The smell of hamburgers and beer on her breath. That is what I remember," he said.

So even though we had very different childhoods, we had some shared experiences. I was so impressed with Milton's thirst for knowledge. He was quite brilliant and he wanted to learn everything there was to know about music, gardening, science, and engineering. You could ask him a question about anything—history, psychology, auto repair—and he'd almost always know the answer. If he didn't, he'd find out. He loved to do research; he was very scholarly. He was the guy people went to for help and answers. He also had an incredible work ethic. If there was a job on campus, he had it. He worked in the cafeteria, he worked in the library, and he mowed the college's lawns. He even had a job off campus at Welch's grape factory.

Somehow through the jobs, the music, the schoolwork, we fell in love. In my senior year, a package arrived at my dorm—it was from Milton, who was living in Queens while studying for his master's in education at Columbia University. It was a 45 rpm record of Sam Cooke singing "You Send Me." I had heard the song about infatuation turned into love many times before, but I'd never really listened closely to the lyrics. In the middle of the song, Sam Cooke sings about wanting to marry his love.

*Wait a minute! Did Milton just propose?*

A few minutes later, Milton called to see if I received the package. "Did you know I just proposed to you?" he asked.

Without hesitation, I said, "*Yes!*" After all, it was a long-distance phone call and it cost money!

I graduated in June 1960 and we married on August 20. We were together for almost forty-six years until his sudden death of pancreatitis on January 17, 2006.

I think our marriage worked because we trusted each other completely. We had such mutual respect and similar goals on what we wanted for our family, our life. We shared the same philosophy on raising kids. Did we agree on everything? Of course not! But the children never saw us in conflict—although behind the scenes we'd have disagreements and discussions. Who doesn't?

Milton was a special, special man. There was no one else like him. We had a good life.

My husband, Milton Williams, with a fellow classmate at a SUNY Fredonia dance. From dancing feet to Latin rhythm to shaking his groove thing, Milton was a great dancer!

Here comes the bride! Debbie and Gretta getting me ready for the walk down the aisle

## CHAPTER 12

*The problem with Vanessa and men is that her father set such a high standard. He was so loving, so trusting, so open-minded, and so smart. He was not a person who could be easily duplicated. I think Vanessa has been searching for a man like her father most of her life.*

—HELEN WILLIAMS

After Mom caught Bruce and me on the pullout sofa, she didn't speak to me for weeks. She was so furious. When she finally did talk, she'd say I was ruining my life. She was afraid I wouldn't graduate from high school.

Why would she worry? So I was rebellious and a risk taker. But I was a good student. There was no reason to worry.

And then . . .

I was a senior in high school when I realized I hadn't gotten my period in more than a month. One January day after school, while my parents were still at work, I snuck into their bedroom and pulled a woman's health book from the bookshelf behind their bed. I flipped through it until I found the chapter on pregnancy. I discovered with horror that I had all the symptoms. I was tired. My breasts were sore and swelling. I had been feeling a little queasy.

YIKES!

I called Bruce and told him that I thought I was pregnant.

"Don't worry. We'll handle this together," he said.

But of course I was worried! And scared. I tried to keep it together. I went to my job at Discovery in Fashion. I went to school. I went to band, orchestra, chorus, and acting rehearsals. The regular routine.

Bruce got the pregnancy test. It was positive.

Shit!

Bruce made an appointment through Planned Parenthood with a doctor in White Plains to "take care of it." Bruce and I didn't think about options. We felt there wasn't a decision to make. We were madly in love, but we were not prepared to be parents or get married. It was all so scary to me. If we had been brave, we would have gotten married and had the child. But we weren't even brave enough to tell my parents. The tragic twist was that we had always talked about marriage and kids. But not in high school!

This was the only alternative. There was nothing else I thought we could do.

I told my mother I had a rehearsal for a show at school. Then I confessed to my acting teacher and asked if he would cover for me while I became a grown-up.

Bruce drove in from New York University (he transferred there his sophomore year to be closer to me). We met in the Greeley parking lot on a cold January afternoon. Then we drove fifteen minutes south to the doctor's office in White Plains. (This Catholic girl was walking into a clinic on Church Street to commit a sin. Major guilt!)

Bruce held my hand as we walked in as a couple. We sat in the waiting room. Then they called my name (I forget which name I used). I stood, let go of Bruce's hand, and a nurse walked me into a small room where I had my procedure—anesthesia, cramping, the sound of the suction machine. Then the life we had talked about was gone. It was awful, terrifying, and just plain sad. It takes a lot of courage to make the other choice. Bruce came in the room to walk me out. Our bond was stronger than ever.

A few years later, when I was Miss America, I said I was pro-choice. "A woman should have the right to make decisions regarding *her* body," I said.

When I was eight weeks pregnant with Melanie, my oldest, I had my first ultrasound. It was a new thing in 1986. I was in awe as I watched this tiny image flicker on the screen. The doctor pointed to what looked like a pulsating grain of rice.

"That's her heart."

I watched the image and listened to the *swish-swish* sound of my baby's heartbeat. I could see life at eight weeks. It was clear—in black and white—that this would be my child. Thank God, he gave me another chance!

I'm still pro-choice—every woman should have the right to choose what she wants to do with her body. I'm still a practicing Catholic. Yes, I did confess, and I'm grateful for the opportunity of forgiveness. I go to church almost every Sunday and pray before I go to bed every night (like my dad taught me). I even have loving priest friends who have guided and helped me through many struggles in life.

But each time I go by that building on Church Street in White Plains, it always takes me back to that cold January day years and years ago. I still get a twinge in the pit of my stomach.

I never directly told Mom about my abortion, but I had a sense she somehow knew. She seemed so disappointed with me, so sad. I often wondered if she went to school that day and found out that there was no rehearsal. If she did, she never said anything to me.

But I believe she knew in her heart. It's a mother's intuition.

## HELEN ON HER SUSPICIONS

Until I read these pages, I didn't know this had happened. I always had my suspicions and I always thought it may have happened, but I didn't know for sure until now. If I think about it hard, I can probably figure out exactly when this happened. As I mentioned, those years had been extremely difficult. But as I read these pages, I realize that the book title can apply to me because in many cases, I had no idea!

Bruce proposed while I was a freshman in college. We'd been through so much together and it just seemed like the right thing at the time. We didn't set a wedding date but dreamed of eloping to Europe. We were ready to start our life together. We were both at Syracuse University. (He had again transferred to be close to me for his junior year—and my parents were furious about this!) He gave me a diamond ring that he had saved up for all summer.

I wore the ring to the kitchen table during my first visit home from Syracuse.

Of course Mom noticed. She notices *everything*. Mom freaked out, but she tried not to show it.

"So, are you planning on getting married now?" she asked with an edge to her voice.

"Not anytime soon."

Mom couldn't hide her disgust and anger. I could practically see the smoke coming out of her ears. She banged around the kitchen and didn't say anything more about it, but I knew she thought I was throwing my life away. She believed I had talent and a great career ahead of me—and I was sacrificing it all for Bruce.

Bruce and I were madly in love. We had such a deep, deep connection—one of those things that only seems possible with your first love. But sometimes I felt like I was suffocating. We took a break the following summer (that summer of the scandalous photos). The break didn't last long. We were a couple again for my sophomore year at Syracuse, where we lived together in a railroad apartment.

Bruce supported everything I did—always sitting as close to the stage as possible—whether it was a play, a dance recital, or my trio of pageants. When I traveled for Miss America, I wasn't supposed to have visits from my boyfriend. But Bruce would sometimes drive nine hours from Syracuse to wherever I was, just to sneak into my room for a few minutes when my chaperones weren't looking. We'd only spend a little time together before I was off to another engagement.

After the news of the photos broke, Bruce was there for me, too. But then I was sequestered at Dennis's house, plotting strategies with Ramon.

We didn't break up in some dramatic way—compared with all the drama in my life at the time. There were no fights or angry words or tears. But I was consumed with the scandal, in seclusion, and figuring out the next phase of my life. Bruce was in school at Syracuse. I couldn't go back there. So he went away. And Ramon and I got closer.

Bruce was my first love and will always have a special place in my heart.

But it was time to move on.

*Bruce and I dining at Maxwell's Plum in New York City, but now as Miss America*

January 28, 1981

THE LOVE CONTRACT

I, Vanessa Williams, hereby agree to all the
following clauses in the Love Contract.

I.   I will continue to love Bruce Hanson forever.

II.  I will never stop loving Bruce Hanson for any reason
     or under any circunstance.

III. I will never leave Bruce Hanson for anyone or anything
     else.

IV.  I will continue to be partners for life, be it love,
     happiness, wealth, or family, with Bruce Hanson.

V.   I agree that he is the best thing to ever happen to me,
     and I to him.

Signed *Vanessa Lynne Williams (Hanson)*

*Crazy in love!*

*Bruce and I posing for a Syracuse photography project on campus*

I was busy cooking a special dinner for Chris, who was home for the first time since starting his freshman year at Georgetown University a few months earlier. Ramon walked into the kitchen and stood next to me, not saying much, but I could tell he had something important to tell me.

*Uh oh.* The alarm went off in my head.

"Yes?" I asked as calmly as possible, but I was not feeling calm at all. My stomach tensed up.

"I would like to marry your daughter and I'm coming to get your blessing."

I looked at him and said flatly: "Well, does Vanessa know about this? Does she want to marry you?"

That's all I said. Ramon looked shocked.

I guess that wasn't exactly the reaction he was hoping for. I truly doubt he was expecting hugs and kisses from me, but I think he was hoping for something a little better than my response. I don't think Ramon ever knew what to make of Milton and me. Ramon told me later that he asked Milton for Vanessa's hand while Milton was underneath the car, fixing something. Milton's response? "You better go talk to Helen."

He never even got out from underneath the car! As you can guess, we weren't happy about it.

Ramon was a very smart, nice guy, who had offered incredible support when Vanessa needed it. I don't think she could have gotten through the Miss America scandal without him. He really came in and saved the day. And Vanessa's always been a romantic. I could see how she could fall in love with him. He was her knight in shining armor.

But does that mean she should marry him?

I learned a long time ago to keep my mouth closed. Vanessa would do what she wanted to do. There was nothing I could say to change that.

But she was only twenty-three years old! (And, as I found out later, pregnant!)

Just a few weeks later—before I could even get used to the idea—I was sitting in a limo with Vanessa and her bridesmaids, Deborah, Toni, and Diane. We were parked out front of the Church of St. Francis Xavier in lower Manhattan, waiting to head in for the wedding. I looked fabulous in a beautiful cranberry-colored Stephen Yearick gown. I was thinking, *I better say something now before it's too late.*

I cleared my throat.

"You still have time. You don't have to get married."

Before I had spoken, everybody had been laughing and chatting. Now there was complete silence. I think I really shocked everyone. Vanessa's and her friends' eyes seemed to pop out. They looked traumatized. They probably had thought I was going to say how happy I was for Vanessa. I just wanted her to know that if she had second thoughts, her father and I were fine with it. We'd be there for her.

Minutes ticked by. It was completely quiet.

Suddenly, Milton was outside the limo, waiting for me.

"Oh, there's Mr. Williams. Mr. Williams is here," the bridesmaids announced as cheerfully as possible.

That was my cue to leave. They just wanted me out of that car as soon as possible. I'm sure the minute the door slammed, they had a conversation about me.

*"Can you believe my mother?"*

But I had to say it. And I'm glad I did. Vanessa was so young. She had her whole life ahead of her. I suppose you could say, who am I to speak? I married Milton when I was only twenty—three years younger than Vanessa was. But that's why I'm the perfect person to speak—I'm talking from experience.

I don't regret marrying Milton one bit. But I had left a family situation that was a disaster, gone to college, graduated, and then got married by age twenty. I never lived on my own or made decisions on my own without taking someone else into consideration. I always felt that being on your own for a while is a very important part of growing up.

If I were to advise a young woman, I'd say, "Be independent for a while. Have your own apartment. Have a career. Get to know who you are first before you get married and start a family and commit to a life of always sharing."

I felt Vanessa was missing out on so much of this. She went from home to Syracuse (where she was with Bruce) to Miss America to Ramon.

Now as a widow, I'm living my life in reverse. For the first time, I'm independent. I'm living by myself. I'm making my own decisions.

Trust me, I wish I could have done it the other way around. But life has its own script, and you have no control.

# CHAPTER 14

*Why get married? Just live together!*

—HELEN WILLIAMS

We were eating at a small, trendy restaurant in SoHo in lower Manhattan when Ramon handed me a poem he'd written about me, our relationship, our love. When I finished the poem, I saw a beautiful antique (from 1899), round-cut diamond ring. Ramon had slipped it under the piece of paper while I was reading. He took my hand and stared into my eyes.

"Will you marry me?"

"Yes!" I cried.

The restaurant burst into applause. It was such a romantic moment.

I had been really surprised. I knew we were going to get married. At the time, we'd been together for one year and had talked about it. We picked out the ring together in Briarcliff Manor at the jewelry store next to my favorite bakery, which made my birthday cake each year (a chocolate cake with fresh strawberries and whipped cream).

After he proposed I moved out to Los Angeles to start my career and live with him.

But we didn't set a wedding date. We said we'd wait until my career took off.

Then on a weekend vacation up the coast to Monterey, California, I became pregnant at twenty-three. When we realized what had happened, we decided, *Okay, we're going to do this now. There's never going to be a perfect time.*

Later, I called to tell my mom that we were going to get married as soon as possible because a bundle of joy was on the way.

A pause. And then . . .

"Why get married? Just live together!"

WHAT? Here we go again!

"And you're pregnant. You're really prepared to do this?"

I was like this rebellious traditionalist. Here was my mom suggesting I just shack up with Ramon for a while. And I said, "We're going to do this and get married and have this child."

I couldn't understand why Mom wasn't happy for me. I was marrying a man who had saved me. A black man—just like she wanted. Why was there always a problem? What was wrong this time?

Even when I told my friends I was engaged the year before, they all wanted to know my mom's reaction. "I can't wait to hear what Helen's going to say about this." "What did Helen say?" My mom's opinion always mattered to people, probably because she never held back.

But despite Mom's reservations, marrying Ramon seemed like the right thing to do. We were in love. Yes, I was young, but I'd lived through so much more than most twentysomethings. In some ways I felt very mature. The thirteen-year age difference didn't seem like a big deal.

My original dream had been to establish a career, get married at twenty-eight, and have children at thirty. I wanted to have a strong career and then a family. I was learning that you can't always make plans.

We were married in front of two hundred friends and relatives at the Church of St. Francis Xavier on Sixteenth Street in Manhattan on January 3, 1987. I wore an ivory-colored silk gown with a six-foot train by Stephen Yearick, who had designed many of my Miss America gowns. You couldn't tell that I was three months pregnant, except for my voluptuous boobs, bursting out of my square neckline.

It was a beautiful wedding. I was marrying my knight in shining armor who had rescued me, the damsel in distress. We had already been through so much together that our marriage could survive just about everything. I was going to prove Mom wrong. I would make this marriage work.

As the white Volvo stretch limo pulled up to the snowy stone stairs, my mom turned to me to say I still had time to change my mind. My bridesmaids, Deborah, Diane, and Toni, still remember that to this day—classic Helen!

But at the reception Mom came up to me, the concern that had consumed her face had vanished.

"Congratulations. I'm happy for you, Ness," Mom said. Then she smiled and hugged me.

WHAT?

Something changed in Mom that day. Up until she stepped out of the limousine in front of the church, she was opposed to my marriage because I was too young—like she had been. She seemed angry. She told me that I didn't have to go through with the wedding. It was Mom's way of saying she didn't approve.

Then after the ceremony, she was a different person. She was happy for me. She let all her concerns, her disappointments, and her anger just evaporate. She understood that I was making my life with Ramon and she could either fight it or be a part of it. It was a turning point for me. Mom finally stopped judging my decisions and accepted me as an adult.

And then I flashed on to something my father had said to me a few years earlier, when I had just moved into my way-too-expensive apartment in Manhattan. It was nearly Christmas, and I had bought my first Christmas tree and decorated it. My parents were visiting. I don't remember the conversation we were having—perhaps my mother and I had been arguing or there was tension in the air. But my father turned to me and very solemnly said, "You have to forgive us for being your parents."

At the time, I had thought to myself, *What made him say that? Was it my hostility?* It had been a stressful, hard time. I was trying to make it on my own after Miss America. I had moved out and I was tired of my parents'—mostly my mom's—judgments. When you're a teenager—and even into your twenties—it's easy to resent everything about your parents. You're trying to break away but part of you still feels very dependent on them and very much influenced by their opinions.

Suddenly I understood—I had to get rid of the anger and resentment I'd bottled up against my mother just because she was being a mother.


We lived in the two-bedroom apartment that Ramon had rented for $700 a month in the Ladera Heights section of Los Angeles, the same one I'd moved into during the summer of 1985. It was a spacious place with a wonderful view of the city. Ramon has great taste and was and is a neat freak.

On Monday morning, June 29, 1987, I woke up with a dull pain in my back.

"I think I'm in labor," I told Ramon.

We were very calm. I didn't want to go to the hospital, so we stayed at home as long as possible. Ramon timed my contractions

## HELEN ON PREMARITAL SLEEPING ARRANGEMENTS

After their honeymoon, Ramon and Vanessa came to the house to visit. Ramon looked at me and smiled. "Now I can sleep in the same bed with my wife." Whenever Vanessa and Ramon stayed with us before they married—even though we knew they lived together in Los Angeles—we wouldn't let them sleep in the same room. It was our house. Our rule. No arguing. 'Nuff said!

while I got a bag together and took a warm shower. I wasn't scared at all, but the pain was uncomfortable. My mother-in-law, Winnie, stayed with me most of the day.

"Let's go!" I finally said.

In the early evening, we drove to Cedars-Sinai.

When we got to the hospital, Dr. Judith Reichman, the most impeccably dressed doctor on the planet, asked if I wanted an epidural.

"Yes!" I was coping but wanted to enjoy the experience instead of cursing Ramon for getting me in this situation and then sneaking peeks of the Lakers' playoff games. So much for natural childbirth!

I gave birth to Melanie Lynne at 2:52 in the morning of June 30, 1987.

From the moment we brought her home, Melanie slept in bed with us—usually on top of one of us. She needed to feel skin on her all the time or she'd cry and wouldn't stop. From 5:30 to 7:30 every night, she was colicky. We tried everything. We'd turn the dryer on and put her on top, praying that the vibration would lull her to sleep. We'd get in the car and just drive and drive, hoping the motion would calm her. She had pacifiers everywhere, in every room, on both sides of our bed. She had this piercing cry that we just couldn't figure out how to stop.

And that's when my relationship with my parents took another turn: Instead of ignoring their advice, I was seeking it. I was breastfeeding, up most of the night and exhausted a lot, but also loving being a new mom. When I struggled to make it through the day, I thought, *Wow, my mom did this, too. She was this career woman who never had any help—just a babysitter while she was at school. She'd work all day and come home and take care of me all night. How did she do it?*

I'd get on the phone nearly every day and ask my mom or dad for some type of baby advice: How do I get her to stop crying? How do I get her to sleep? Should I give her solid food yet?

Ramon and I didn't have a nanny or even an occasional babysitter, so I'd take Melanie everywhere with me—to auditions and recording sessions. During auditions other actresses would watch her in her stroller while I went in to read for a role. I was being sent on lots and lots of auditions, but I wasn't booking any work.

When I had lived in New York, my first professional theater role was an off-Broadway musical called *One Man Band* at the South Street Theater, a ninety-nine-seat house on Theatre Row. I played a muse in the background along with Judy Gibson and Kay Cole. It became such a hot ticket that summer of 1985 that Andy Warhol, Magic Johnson, and other celebs stopped by to see it (Andy came backstage to meet me afterward and barely said a peep). Debra Barsha, the show's musical director, had moved to Los Angeles around the same time as I had. One day she called me.

"I'm doing this gig with George Clinton. Do you know who he is? Do you want to sing backup with me?" she asked.

What? Of course I knew George Clinton—George Clinton & Parliament Funkadelic!

*"With One Look"*
Sister Sandra and me—notice my expression. It means hurry up and take this photo or else you will end up on "the List!"

*"Always on My Mind"*
My sister Gretta. I miss her so much.

*"Chopsticks"*
From an early age I always knew music would play a major role in my life.

*"Everlasting Love"*
Milton, at his base camp while stationed in Korea, missing me.

*"My Endless Love"*
And so the journey begins

*"It's My Time to Be Blessed"*
Mrs. Milton A. Williams Jr.

*"Love Will Never Change"*
Buffalo, New York, August 20, 1960

Since the night of the live telecast, this gown has taken on a life of its own! Last check it was on display at a fashion museum near Syracuse University.

In the VIP suite with my mom, dad, and brother, Chris. This photo appeared in dozens of newspapers across the country the morning after the pageant.

Walking down the aisle of St. Francis Xavier with my dad

Afterglow with Toni, Deborah, and Diane

Dad, Ramon, Mom, and my brother, Chris

NAACP Image Award for Outstanding
Supporting Actress in a Comedy Series
as Wilhelmina Slater on *Ugly Betty*, Los
Angeles, 2007

With my mom on the red carpet at the Academy
Awards the night "Colors of the Wind" won the
Oscar for Best Original Song, 1996

Pregnant with Devin at the Grammys, after performing "Save the Best for Last," Los Angeles, 1993

Doing tango during a dress rehearsal for *Kiss of the Spider Woman* on Broadway, 1994

"Where You Are" with my boys, as Aurora in *Kiss of the Spider Woman*, 1994

*Into the Woods* curtain
call with John McMartin
on Broadway, 2002

With Rick Valenzuela
at the International
Ballroom Champion-
ships, Boston, 1998

Performing the national anthem at Super Bowl XXX in Tempe, Arizona (Steelers vs. Cowboys), January 1996

With my fabulous band and crew on our national tour with Luther Vandross, 1997

*Vanessa Williams & Friends: Christmas in New York* TV special with Luther Vandross and Shania Twain, 1996

Christmas concert with Plácido Domingo and Tony Bennett, in Vienna, 2000

Me and Mom in Chicago with megamogul Oprah Winfrey

Sting surprised me in the studio with background vocals when I covered "Sister Moon."

At the Jackie Robinson Awards honoring the legendary Lena Horne, New York, 1984

Arnold presented me with the Lena Horne Award at the Soul Train Music Awards, Los Angeles, 1996

Always classy and elegant, the legendary Diahann Carroll played my mother in *The Courage to Love*, on location in Canada, 1999.

And the sizzling siren Eartha Kitt played my mom in *And Then Came Love*, New York, 2006.

Showered with rose petals on the steps of the Church of the Holy Trinity in New York City, 1999

Listening to Kenny Lattimore serenade us during our first dance

Both families joined in matrimony

With the family at my Hollywood Walk of Fame star ceremony in front of the historic Hollywood Roosevelt hotel—a big day! 2007

Finally! My graduation ceremony from Syracuse University, Mother's Day Weekend, 2008

Devin's confirmation at Saint John and Saint Mary, (left to right) Jillian, Mom, Sasha, Devin, me, Melanie, and Ramon, 2009

Mom's seventieth birthday bash in New York, wearing her favorite color: red, December 2009

Christmas with Mom, Dad, Devin, Jillian, and my favorite uncle, Earl, December 1994

Christmas in Marina del Rey, California, 2000

Wilhelmina on the rooftop before she gets busy with a baseball bat, Los Angeles, 2008

*Mode* Rules! With my costars on *Ugly Betty*, Michael Urie and Becki Newton, Los Angeles, 2009

A moment of calm before the scene where Wilhelmina has to torment the lovely Betty White, Los Angeles, 2007

Wilhelmina marries Bradford on my actual anniversary to Rick, who was guest starring in that episode . . . crazy! Los Angeles, September 2007

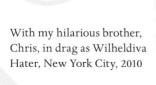

With my hilarious brother, Chris, in drag as Wilheldiva Hater, New York City, 2010

With Team *Ugly Betty* after winning Best Comedy Series at the Golden Globe Awards in Beverly Hills, January 2007

Guess who's comin' to stir up some trouble on Wisteria Lane . . . me! 2010

Final season as Renee Perry on *Desperate Housewives*, 2012

"Yes!"

George Clinton was doing a solo project. I went to his studio in Hollywood and the man with the craziest hair greeted me. What a blast! I had danced to "Flashlight" at high school parties and here I was reading his handwriting on lined paper with his lyrics to new songs. Then George sang the parts he wanted me to sing and I sang them back to him. I was being produced by an R & B legend while he snacked on cold eggs. I ended up singing background on two songs on his 1986 album *R&B Skeletons in the Closet*—"Do Fries Go with That Shake?" and "Hey Good Lookin'."

Afterward he wanted to sign me to a production deal. We went to see Prince together to get songs for the project. He gave me two songs on a cassette (which I can't find to save my life). Prince met us backstage at the Universal Amphitheatre. He saw me, and George said, "This is Vanessa." Then he saw Ramon and said, "Oh, I forgot." We never recorded the two songs. I guess since I wasn't romantically available, I also became professionally unavailable. But the meeting was thrilling.

Working with George Clinton had given me some street cred. Most record companies don't want to hear from you if your background is in theater. That's cornball city to them. They were looking for singers with raspy voices, which I didn't have. "Do Fries Go with That Shake?" turned out to be the second-highest charting single of George's solo career, peaking at number thirteen on the Billboard Hot Black Singles chart.

That got me a dinner meeting with Ed Eckstine, who'd just been named general manager of Wing Records—a small, new record label that was part of PolyGram. At Columbia Records I had met with Benny Medina, who wanted to sign me to a production deal. But it was Ed who said, "Let's make you an artist."

Ed and I hit it off right away and he signed me to the label. Ed had a great sense of humor and was really smart. Besides having similar musical tastes, Ed and I looked like we could be from the same tribe. With his light black skin and blue eyes, he could have been my long-lost cousin. He was ten years older than me, so he wasn't the guy in a suit behind a huge desk smoking a cigar. Ed, the son of popular singer Billy Eckstine, was hungry to make a name for himself and the division. He'd spent years working under Quincy Jones and now he was on his own.

Ed had something to prove. I had something to prove. Ramon, as my new manager, had something to prove. When everyone has something to prove, that's when magic happens.

Still, it was a struggle getting music. The big-name pop writers assumed I would be a flash in the pan. Back then, the record labels all had an A & R department—Artists and Repertoire—so Ed had a team of people poring through the tapes that were sent in. We listened to all the hungry young writers looking for their big break. I didn't want to discount anything because you never know when you'll find the jewels. We loved to find the people who hadn't had the shot but were tremendously talented.

One time the UPS guy was delivering something to my house. He knew I was recording an album and he handed me a cassette.

"Will you give this a listen?" he asked.

I threw it in the car along with all the other cassettes I'd collected. Then I popped it into the player while I was driving. "Can This Be Real?" was a beautiful ballad that I knew would be perfect for my voice. I ended up including it on my first album, *The Right Stuff*, all thanks to the UPS guy.

Kenny "Babyface" Edmonds and L.A. Reid, both singers and songwriters (who would later become producers), had just moved to Los Angeles from Cincinnati. Ed had called them and they said they had a song called "Girlfriend." I listened to it at Ed's office and then met with them in their small two-bedroom apartment/studio on Highland Avenue. They played the song for me on an electric piano. The song had a lot of attitude—a great hook and it screamed R & B hit. While we sang it through at the piano, a younger singer named Pebbles walked into the apartment.

"Wow, that's the jam," she said when I finished.

"I know," I said.

"No, that's the jam," she said again.

"Yeah, I know."

Hmmm . . . You know how this ended up.

"Girlfriend" became Pebbles's first single from her platinum-selling album. Pebbles also eventually married L.A. Reid. They're now divorced and she's an ordained minister.

I couldn't focus on these setbacks since most of my days were spent taking care of Melanie and adjusting to motherhood. I loved being a mom, and it came naturally for me—maybe because I had babysat a lot of the children in our neighborhood when I was growing up.

Dad would always say, "Just let kids explore. Let them figure things out on their own and test their limits. Don't give them fear." Melanie and I would take long walks together in the neighborhood and go to Mommy and Me classes at My Gym. Even as a baby she was a very dreamlike, expressive child. Sometimes we'd curl up on the couch and watch videos of ballets and musicals. Melanie could watch an entire performance of *Swan Lake* and be fascinated. She also loved *Singin' in the Rain*.

My career was focused on recording. The routine was that when Ramon came home from work, I'd jump in the car and head out to a small studio in the back of a house in Toluca Lake. I'd work late into the night—and sometimes into the morning—putting together *The Right Stuff*. It was a very relaxed atmosphere, although I knew there was a lot on the line.

In the summer of 1988, "The Right Stuff" single came out at the same time as my labelmate Nia Peeples released *Nothin' But Trouble*.

She was already well-known for her role as Nicole Chapman on the television show *Fame*. So the focus at the label was on her. They invested their sales and marketing efforts in her album.

The inside word was: *Don't get excited about Vanessa, Nia's the one to watch.*

Business Affairs saw me as a one-hit wonder. They thought I'd have this one album, garner a bit of interest from the public because of my Miss America past, and then disappear for good.

I was getting used to being discounted so immediately. "You're a beauty queen? Now you're a recording artist? Yeah, right." But I knew I had to show people that I was more than the headlines. I had such great support from Ramon and my parents. Growing up, when my parents discovered I had talent, they never discouraged me or suggested I have a backup plan. They never said, "Get a real job!" They told me I could do it. "Work hard, do your best, and live your dream," they said. So I never had any doubts. Besides, being the underdog is something I thrive on. It pushes me to excel. After all, success is the sweetest revenge. I was determined to make this album work.

Ramon, Ed, and I all knew there was a lot of pressure to have a successful first album. In the record business, you rarely—if ever—get a second chance.

When I went on the road to promote the album, Ramon and Melanie came with me. The record company had me scheduled for radio station interviews, track dates (where you sing live to your taped music), summer festivals, you name it—anywhere I could get my R & B audience to hear my music. We were a family on the road: Mom up front, Dad managing from behind, and Melanie tagging along and wiggling to my music in her car seat on our cross-country adventure.

We'd drive from one town to the next—meeting with program directors and praying the single would climb the charts. We'd hit every local R & B station and then pop stations. I'd do radio interviews, sit in as a guest deejay for Tom Joyner, pose for photos with program directors. I'd appear at record store signings (thank God the lines were long—there's nothing worse than the fear that no one will show up). I'd introduce acts like Paula Abdul, En Vogue, and New Kids on the Block at the big outdoor festivals in major cities. Paula Abdul and I performed together in Indiana and on *Showtime at the Apollo*. (Years later, when "Save the Best for Last" hit number one, Paula sent me flowers and a congratulatory note, which I thought was very classy of her, since earlier her album had soared past mine—and gone multiplatinum).

After we were done stateside, we hopped on a plane and traveled abroad through Germany, England, France, Australia, and Japan.

It paid off. "The Right Stuff" was the first single released and it hit number four on *Billboard's* R & B chart, followed by "(He's Got) The Look," which hit number ten. "Dreamin'" reached number one on the R & B chart and hit number eight on the singles chart.

## HELEN'S RIGHT STUFF

Vanessa called us one day to say that she was nominated for Grammys. She was so excited and we were thrilled. "The Right Stuff" was one of my favorites, especially the video because it highlighted her dancing skills so well. All those years of dance classes were finally paying off! Of course we thought she should win everything. When she didn't, we were just happy she was getting the recognition she deserved.

The album eventually sold more than 500,000 copies and went gold. It earned two Grammy nominations, and I was nominated in the Best New Artist category!

But with each success, I didn't feel like I could relax. I still had so much to prove. When the first song was a hit, people would say it was just because the media was curious and I got more press than I really deserved. When the second song did well, the attitude was "Hmmm, she got lucky. But can she do it again?"

I did it again.

There was this premise set up that because I was a former beauty queen—a scandalous beauty queen—I was getting more attention than I should have.

Journalists could not get past the scandal. I'd be interviewed about my music, but in my head, I'd be ticking off the minutes until the Question would come up. I'd think, *Okay, when is "it" coming?* I could almost predict it. They'd ask me the album questions, the family questions, and then right before the interview was over, they'd slip in some kind of scandal question. At first I'd feel blindsided by it.

One time right before Melanie was born, a reporter said, "Congratulations! You're married and you're having a baby!" I smiled and said, "Thank you."

"So, what will you tell your child about the scandal?"

What? Are you kidding me? My baby hasn't even been born yet!

No matter what I did, I was always reduced to those photos.

When I became Miss America, I was twenty, freethinking, and optimistic. By twenty-one, I had become really guarded. I had to be a tough chick, always ready to be on the defensive and shut people down.

Early on, just as I was starting my career as an actress, Bryant Gumbel, then one of the *Today* show hosts, interviewed me about a

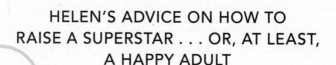

## HELEN'S ADVICE ON HOW TO RAISE A SUPERSTAR . . . OR, AT LEAST, A HAPPY ADULT

- Give your child as many opportunities as you can. You expose them to as much as possible.
- Let them participate in as many activities as they can handle—but don't push your own agenda.
- If they have a good singing voice, let it develop naturally. Too many parents force their children into voice lessons when they're not ready. They develop a sound that doesn't suit them and often ruin their vocal cords in the process.
- Allow your children to find their own strengths and paths in life. Never discourage them—even if it's not what you want them to do (unless it's something illegal).

guest role on *Partners in Crime*, a show starring Loni Anderson and Lynda Carter. We had an agreement with the producers beforehand that Bryant wouldn't ask me any questions about Miss America. As we were wrapping up the interview, Bryant said, "What do you think of this?" Then they rolled a clip of Bob Guccione stating that the *Penthouse* scandal made my career. (Of course it hadn't!) NBC technically didn't ask about Miss America but they snuck it in through the back door. And you wonder why I had trust issues with the media.

I remember shopping for my first car in Los Angeles—a Saab. Mark, the salesman, congratulated me on the album and I said to him, "Okay. When is this going to hit me? Should I feel something right now?" My album was selling, but I hadn't made any money yet. I learned that a record company operated just like a bank. All the money they'd pumped into promoting my album came out of my pockets. Promotion, road costs, videos—they all get recouped by the label before you see any real money. I was waiting for my payday.

And then my album finally went gold, but all I could think was *Why hadn't it gone platinum?* Paula Abdul, Nia Peeples, and Pebbles all had albums that debuted when mine did—and theirs had all gone platinum. Why hadn't mine?

I never stopped and just enjoyed the fact that going gold was pretty great. I wanted more. I had so much more to do and prove. Even while I was listening to my songs being played on the radio, I had to think about my next album. I had to make an even better follow-up album to show everyone that what I'd just accomplished wasn't some type of fluke.

I had so much more work to do.

On location in San Francisco for my first acting job after resigning as Miss America, here as Rosselle Robinson on the NBC show PARTNERS IN CRIME, starring Loni Anderson and Lynda Carter

I was almost in Spike Lee's SCHOOL DAZE, but Melanie's in my tummy.

In Malibu with Richard Pryor for ANOTHER YOU

*Studio time with Chaka Khan and the gang*

*(clockwise) Lynn Whitfield, Vanessa Bell Calloway, Jasmine Guy, and me in* STOMPIN' AT THE SAVOY

*Singing "La Vie en Rose" as Josephine Baker for* MOTOWN RETURNS TO THE APOLLO

# CHAPTER
## 15

*You can't have your husband also be your manager because something will suffer—either your marriage or your career. You need to have a bit of a break from each other.*

—HELEN WILLIAMS

All my children were conceived on vacations, so I shouldn't have been surprised when I returned from a trip to the Exumas in the Bahamas and discovered I was pregnant.

Ramon and I were thrilled. I loved creating a family. I'd grown up with parents who believed that marriage and children were the most important things. I know a lot of people feel that a family can get in the way of a career, especially when you're starting out. But I felt the opposite—creating a family gave me something else to focus on. I wasn't consumed with my career. I couldn't become self-absorbed because I was too busy changing diapers.

We were living in a house in Playa del Rey, a seaside town southwest of Los Angeles, when I went into labor. I hate hospitals. Who doesn't? So I waited until the very last minute to leave the comfort of my home for the sterile, scary environment of a hospital. Guess I waited too long! I thought I was going to give birth right in the Saab. It was a close call. I was squeezing the handle above the window through intense contractions. I was in agony and the contractions were right on top of one another. Ramon raced through the streets and dropped me off at the emergency entrance of Cedars-Sinai.

I checked into triage. Then Dr. Reichman arrived wearing a white linen suit. She told me I was ten centimeters dilated and instructed someone to tell Ramon to hurry parking the car or he was going to miss his baby's birth.

I never made it to the delivery room. I had my baby right in the labor room. Ramon ran in just minutes before I gave birth to Jillian Kristen. She was born at 10:35 in the morning on June 19, 1989.

I had just moved into my hospital room and was being served lunch while Jillian slept in my arms. Ramon, who had called everyone with the news and then left to take care of some business, walked back into the room, carrying a big boom box.

"I need you to do some liners for Japan," he said.

I thought, *WHAT? Now? You're kidding me, right?*

"The deadline is today."

*I just pushed out OUR child a few hours ago!*

I was pissed with Ramon for thinking about business at a time like this. Right then it was clear to me that the line had been blurred between wife and client. I did the work. I'm a pro. But I was so resentful because I just wanted my husband, not my manager, there.

Instead of telling him any of this, I kept it to myself and just did it.

I was building a lot of pent-up frustration toward Ramon because he didn't know how to take off the manager hat and just be a husband, a father. It wasn't completely his fault—I had asked him to manage me. It was *our* fault. Ramon and I didn't have any escape from each other. We were always together and it seemed that, no matter what, it was always about the work. But I also knew he was the only one who saw my potential.

He knew a lot about the biz. And I relied on his knowledge, although control issues had become blurred because of our dual roles as husband/manager and wife/talent.

*I* was supposed to be in control of *my* career, yet I was in my twenties and raising a family. I couldn't possibly do it all. I'd let Ramon be in charge of my career and our money because it was too much to handle. But I didn't feel like I had any control whatsoever.

Jillian was only eight weeks old when Ramon and I headed to Glasgow to promote *The Right Stuff* in Great Britain. It was my first time away from my newborn and two-year-old Melanie. We hired a grandmother-type nanny. Ramon felt pressure from the European label to expose me to the worldwide market, but I desperately wanted to stay home. Two weeks is a long time to be away from a newborn. I was nursing, swollen, bleeding. Plus, I would miss milestones in her brand-new life. I had Ramon's family in L.A. to check up on them, but I wanted my babies.

When I went through airport security in Scotland, the screeners pulled my breast pump out of my carry-on bag, looked at it strangely, and asked me what it was. I thought, *Why the hell am I doing this? I'm traveling with a breast pump but no baby!* How do you balance career and motherhood? I had to go; our livelihood depended on it, so there wasn't a choice. My career won that battle.

Now it's hip and sexy to be a mom or have a baby bump, but back then you had to hide it, or at least, not flaunt it. I felt I had to prove I could still do the work despite being a new mom.

As a singer, I was supposed to be sexy and alluring, not an exhausted mother and wife who wanted to stay home and breast-feed.

But I *was* exhausted by the demands of motherhood. In between radio interviews, I pumped my breasts, threw out the milk, and bottled my growing resentments.

When I returned home I began work on my second album, *The*

*Comfort Zone.* Since I'd already had some hits with *The Right Stuff,* it was much easier to find music—publishers submitted songs to Ed for me. But even though the last album went gold, in some ways I felt like I was starting from scratch. I told Ed I didn't want to sing any of those "I can't live without you" or "without you I'm nothing" type songs. They never spoke to me. I never liked lyrics that involved a woman begging and pleading for a man. It wasn't in my constitution. I'm not that girl and never have been.

I didn't want to sing ballads about wimpy girls waiting to find love. I wanted to combine killer dance tunes with rich ballads as well as some familiar tunes. I decided on "What Will I Tell My Heart?" and a remake of the Isley Brothers' "Work to Do."

I still had so much to prove. I had to fill this album with great, great songs.

Legend has it that Barbra Streisand and Bette Midler passed on it, but who knows if that's true. Because when "Save the Best for Last" became a huge hit, everyone was like, "Why didn't I get that song?" No one would ever admit that they didn't hear its potential. But the song had never been intended for me. The writers had shopped it around to a bunch of artists who all said no—until it finally found its way to me.

I'd already had a hit with the ballad "Dreamin'," so when Ed was sent "Save the Best for Last," he knew I could nail it. The song was cowritten by Wendy Waldman (she'd written songs for Crystal Gayle, Aaron Neville, Judy Collins, and Bette Midler, to name a few), who performed the ballad on the demo tape. I listened to this sweet, pure voice accompanied by a piano and simple production and immediately got chills. I knew it was a great song that was unique and not overproduced. The melody line was haunting and powerful and beautiful. To me, that's what makes a song wonderful: It lives with you and you can't get it out of your head—once you absorb it, you can't forget it. The simplicity of a fantastic melody is undeniable. I was hooked.

But I had no idea how big it would be.

Ed had paired me up with Keith Thomas, a writer and producer who was known mostly as a Christian and gospel music producer. Keith had just branched into R & B and had written and recorded "Heaven," a big hit for R & B singers BeBe and CeCe Winans. I loved the song. It was not your usual idea for a gospel song. It was warm, rich, and contemporary but at the same time, very soulful. The first time I heard it, I was blown away. So when Ed set up a meeting, I was very excited to meet Keith.

When Keith walked into Ed's office, Ed and I were both shocked. He was white! Because of the music he'd done, we had just expected him to be black. Ed and I looked at each other and smiled—in front of us was this five-foot-eight white guy with brown curly hair and a thick Southern accent. He was full of life, really excited, and eager for an opportunity to cross over into a more mainstream territory.

Since he'd worked with Quincy Jones for years, Ed had a bunch of what I referred to as Quincyisms. He'd tell me, "Once you cross over you can never get black." Michael Jackson, Lionel Richie, and anyone who was embraced by the pop world after being "made" by the black community had "crossed over." It wasn't necessarily a bad thing. That's where the money is. But at the same time, you don't want to lose your core audience. You want to straddle the color lines and survive. That's the mission. I knew that the R & B audience and urban listeners who had made *The Right Stuff* a hit were black. The task with a sophomore record was to reach a wider audience.

Time for album number two. The girls, our new nanny—Kathi—and I moved into a hotel in Franklin, Tennessee, a tiny town about twenty miles south of downtown Nashville, where Keith had his studio, Yellow Elephant Music, Inc. He had signed on to produce

50 percent of the album—five songs, including "Save the Best for Last."

Franklin (now famous for being Miley Cyrus's hometown) was such a small town that the only place to stay by the studio was a hotel right off the highway. There was a main street with a town square, a quilting store, and a movie theater. I'd record all day and my girls would stop by and visit. It was such a simple and relaxing time. Keith was eager to make hits with me, excited that we could prove ourselves together.

You feel extremely vulnerable when you record a song because you're in a room alone while everyone else is on the other side of the big plate-glass window, listening to every sound that comes out of your mouth. Your voice seems so loud and every sound you make seems amplified. You're singing while taking direction and listening to criticism. Then you take a break and do it all over again, for days and days.

Keith was amazing to work with, and I credit him with really finding my sound. He had a bunch of mikes and I settled on a rebuilt vintage C-22 with a heated tube inside. It has a warm sound and complements my tone. Keith also handed me a big bag of Lay's Potato Chips.

"Chip up."

"Huh?"

"Grab a chip."

Keith's theory was that the oil and salt of the Lay's chips gives your vocal cords a shimmer. He used the chip trick with all his singers.

When *The Comfort Zone* debuted, I was traveling. I sang on television shows in Germany, Hong Kong, Taiwan, and Australia plus all over the States. I was so focused on the work that I hardly noticed that "Save the Best for Last" was steadily climbing up the Billboard charts. It knocked my childhood idol Michael Jackson's "Remember the Time" out of the number one spot on *Billboard*'s pop, rhythm and blues, and adult contemporary singles charts.

The song stayed there for five weeks and pulled my second album into the top twenty.

I was touring and traveling and performing, so there didn't seem to be any time to reflect. I didn't have a chance to savor the success. There wasn't a moment when I jumped up and down and screamed. It was always like, *What's next? How do I top this?*

I did notice that when deejays announced my songs on the radio, they called me "Vanessa Williams, singer," or "Vanessa Williams, pop star." At some point along the way, while my songs were climbing the charts, the public had finally put my scandal in the past.

I was nominated for four Grammy awards. "Save the Best for Last" was up for Best Song; Best Record; and Best Pop Vocal Performance, Female. The song "The Comfort Zone" was nominated for best R & B Vocal Performance, Female.

I was thirty-three weeks pregnant with my third child when I performed "Save the Best for Last" at the 1993 Grammys at the Shrine Auditorium in Los Angeles. I sang while sitting on a stool in a black lace blouse with black chiffon pants. Afterward, while I was still backstage, Bonnie Raitt announced the winner for Best Song. I was up against Eric Clapton's "Tears in Heaven," Billy Ray Cyrus's "Achy Breaky Heart," Celine Dion and Peabo Bryson's "Beauty and the Beast," and k.d. lang's "Constant Craving."

"And the song of the year is . . . 'Tears in Heaven' . . ."

I know it sounds cliché, but it really is an honor just to be nominated; just to be in the same category as a legend like Eric felt great. "Tears in Heaven" was Eric Clapton's beautiful ballad about his four-year-old son, Conor, who had accidentally fallen out of an apartment building window and died.

For five weeks "Tears in Heaven" had been neck and neck with "Save the Best for Last" on the Billboard charts. "Save the Best for

Last" was number one and "Tears in Heaven" was right behind. I had missed Clapton's acceptance speech. When I returned to my seat, Keith excitedly nudged me. "Did you hear what he said? Eric Clapton just talked about you!"

"I think Vanessa Williams should have got it because it kept ["Tears in Heaven"] out of the number one spot for two months," Clapton had said.

Wow!

Even though I didn't win any awards that night, it was pretty cool having Clapton talk about me onstage. Almost as good as a win.

I wasn't an outsider anymore.

CHAPTER

# 16

*Being with her children is when Vanessa's the happiest.*
*Being on the Broadway stage takes a pretty close second.*

—HELEN WILLIAMS

The last few years had been wonderfully successful. Besides having another baby—a boy, Devin Christian (conceived in Devon, England, while promoting *The Comfort Zone*) on April 14, 1993—my 1991 album, *The Comfort Zone,* was a multiplatinum seller. I'd racked up a total of two NAACP Image Awards and seven Grammy award nominations. I'd starred in a few television movies, including *The Kid Who Loved Christmas* and *Stompin' at the Savoy.* I'd had a part in the TV miniseries *The Jacksons: An American Dream.* I'd also appeared in *Another You* with Richard Pryor and Gene Wilder, as well as in *Harley Davidson and the Marlboro Man* with Don Johnson and Mickey Rourke. Plus, I was working on another album, *The Sweetest Days.*

And best of all, we were living in Chappaqua, New York, which was just a few miles from where I grew up. Home! Even though I'd lived in Los Angeles for seven years, I never felt like I belonged. I never felt truly comfortable or at home there. Maybe it's the vibe of transience. Los Angeles is the epicenter of the entertainment industry, so people are always in and out, coming and going. Deep down, I was one of those people, too. I always thought I'd be on the West Coast for three years, at the most. That had been my plan. But it seemed that another day, another month, another year had zoomed by. And suddenly I had been living on the West Coast for seven years.

The last few years in Los Angeles hadn't been easy. I felt like Ramon and I were drifting apart. To break away from just being known as "Vanessa's manager," Ramon had started R&B Live, which showcased African-American pop and R & B performers. Operating out of the 20/20 Club in Century City each Wednesday night, it had quietly built a reputation as the hippest ticket in town for music-industry insiders, Hollywood celebrities, sports stars, and studio executives.

It was a huge success, attracting such talents as Stevie Wonder; Chaka Khan; the Brothers Johnson; Thelma Houston; and Earth, Wind & Fire. Ramon was on top of his game—as a manager and as the creator of R&B Live. But I began to dread Wednesdays because Ramon would disappear all night, sometimes not returning until late the next morning. I had no idea where he was, but I'd be home with two young children and I was pregnant with my third. I'd take the girls to preschool the next day—just as Ramon would be pulling into our driveway.

"Get it together or I'm going back to my parents with the kids," I said.

A few months later on April 29, 1992, Los Angeles was turned into a war zone when a jury acquitted three white cops and one Hispanic cop accused in the videotaped beating of black motorist Rodney King. Ramon, the girls, and I had been on a promotional tour in Germany when the verdict was announced. We saw the chaos on the news but we didn't know what mayhem awaited us. Our plane was diverted to Las Vegas for a while because of the gunfire near the Los Angeles airport. When we finally descended into Los Angeles, you could smell the smoke.

Los Angeles looked like a ghost town enveloped in smoke and flames. I was heartbroken by what had happened and couldn't believe the destruction. As we drove to our home, we passed a gas station and saw the owner standing outside, alone, holding a lead pipe to protect his business. It really felt like the apocalypse had arrived.

It was time to get out, time to start anew. Ramon agreed that we needed a change.

Melanie was nearly five and I'd always planned to be back on the East Coast in time to enroll the girls in kindergarten. I wanted the kids to be raised in a place where they could have a normal life, without the constant glare of Hollywood and all its artifice. I wanted them to appreciate the beauty of the seasons—the colorful array of leaves in the fall; sleigh rides through snow in the winter; the smell of blooming flowers in the spring; fireflies lighting the skies in summer. I wanted them to have the kind of life I knew as a child.

Those were the wishes for my children, but I had some of my own. I wanted to be closer to my parents so they could have a more active, consistent role in the children's lives. After months of searching all over Westchester County—from as far north as South Salem to as far south as Scarsdale—we landed in Chappaqua, just one town over from my old stomping grounds.

When my parents found their Millwood home, they had fallen in love with the property—not the house. I felt the same way when I drove along a windy path toward this turn-of-the-century fieldstone farmhouse. There was a huge, sloping front lawn that had once been a pasture. At the base of the hill were towering evergreens and a row of apple trees (where deer often grazed) as well as a pond filled with ducks and geese. The property—once owned by A. H. Smith, the one-time president of the New York Central Railroad—was beautiful, with so much potential. I imagined putting in a swimming pool, Jacuzzi, and tennis court. I also pictured a beautiful English garden where I could pick my own herbs and flowers.

The property was perfect. The house, however, needed a lot of work.

When we bought the place, there was a guesthouse, a carriage house, and a stone barn, which I knew we'd eventually combine into one house. I didn't know at the time what a daunting task this would actually be. All I knew was that I was finally home.

My career was soaring, I was back east, yet something was missing and I knew exactly what it was. Ever since I was a young girl watching Stephanie Mills light up the stage in *The Wiz*, I wanted to be on Broadway. "See you on Broadway," I'd written in my senior yearbook at Horace Greeley. I wanted to be onstage more than anything, but I was beginning to wonder when this would come to fruition.

I never doubted it would happen, but what was taking so long?

And then the call came. Finally! It was the phone call I always knew I'd get one day.

"*Show Boat* is coming to Broadway and they want you to audition for the part of Julie LaVerne, the leading lady," Emily Gerson-Saines, my agent at William Morris, told me.

I was thrilled. *Show Boat*, a musical by Jerome Kern and Oscar Hammerstein, was being produced and directed by Harold Prince. It had premiered in Toronto with Lonette McKee, an actress and singer, starring in the lead role. It was scheduled to open at the Gershwin Theatre in October. Lonette hadn't signed on for the Broadway run, so the part was available.

I sang "Can't Help Lovin' Dat Man" for Garth Drabinsky, one of the show's producers.

"That was great, wonderful," he told me. "But it looks like Lonette is going to stay with the show after all."

But Garth wasn't finished.

"How about replacing Chita Rivera in *Kiss of the Spider Woman?*"

What? Me, replace the legendary Chita Rivera? It sounded like a dream.

I hadn't seen the show, but I knew the buzz around it. The Harold Prince–directed play had won seven Tony Awards, including Best Musical, Best Performance by a Leading Actor, and Best Performance by a Leading Actress—Chita Rivera. It was the hottest show in town, but the original cast was leaving the production. Chita and the other leads were going on tour with the show.

A few days later I headed to the Broadhurst Theater and was blown away by the show. Chita—at sixty years old—was fantastic. She kicked her legs over her head and spun around the stage. I also loved the premise of the show—Aurora, Chita's character, exists only in the memory of Molina, a gay window dresser who is incarcerated in a Latin American prison. To escape his world, he brings Aurora to life, where she dances and smolders, all in fabulous, colorful costumes.

"This is fantastic. I love it! I can't wait to do it," I told Garth.

I was in rehearsals for three weeks, singing and dancing and feeling more alive than I'd felt in a long time. Theater performers work harder than anyone in the business and the bonds you make with the other actors are immediate and strong. Everyone wants the same thing—to put on a killer show.

Being a recording artist is great, but I never thought I'd have a career as a recording artist. Acting is what I love—what I've always loved. The people—the cast, the crew—are the people I admire and respect the most in the business. When you're rehearsing with stage actors, you almost immediately become family because you just have everything in common. They get your song and dance references; you don't have to explain anything. They have the same work ethic. They value time. They value art. On Broadway, the attitude is "How can I make the scene work best for everyone?" Whereas in film and television, many actors want to make sure they alone look good. Their attitude is "To hell with the scene."

We were rehearsing nonstop. It was exhausting but exhilarating. I performed solos as well as strenuous dance numbers that required harnesses to climb up the prison bars.

I was part of a group of performers—and we all had so much to prove. The original cast had done such an amazing, amazing job, so there was a lot of pressure on us to do just as well or better. Chita was wonderful. I trailed her one night. She was extremely accessible, but if she didn't want to be disturbed she'd put a stuffed gorilla in front of her dressing room door. Then people knew to leave her alone!

I was in a cast with veteran Broadway actors Brian Mitchell (he didn't use Stokes as a middle name yet) and Howard McGillin. We were the "B" team. But instead of just taking over the parts and doing the same show, we got a chance to reinvent it. My interpretation of Aurora was very different from Chita's. We weren't the fifteenth cast of *Chicago* doing the same choreography, the same interpretation. We made it hotter and sexier. The heat onstage was incredible. The male dancers were shirtless most of the time, dancing these passionate tangos while gyrating their hips. I was thirty-one—nearly half Chita's age. Howard McGillin, who had been married, had just come out as a gay man, and he was cast in a flamboyantly gay role. He was proclaiming his sexual identity in the role of Molina. It was steamy, sexy, and hot, hot, hot.

But would it work?

To me, there's nothing scarier than the "put-in." The put-in is the one and only rehearsal where the actors replacing other actors get the opportunity to run through the entire play from start to finish with the full performing company, orchestra, lights, sound, and costume. It is both nerve-racking and a huge adrenaline rush. But it's terrifying because if something doesn't work well, can you really fix it by the next night—opening night?

We'd had only three weeks to rehearse, but the put-in was nearly flawless. We hit all our cues and changed costumes on time. In the first act, my character is in a harness and flown up to the top of the prison during a blackout. I forgot that during the flight offstage, I was supposed to stay in a deep second position—a dance position where my legs are sideways—so I wouldn't bang into the iron bars of the prison. Well, it wasn't deep enough.

OUCH! I whacked my knee all the way up.

When I got off stage my knee was swollen and gushing blood. It was quickly bandaged. Then I changed into a gorgeous Tropicana-like outfit covered with feathers and got back on the stage.

I did the rest of the show in tremendous pain. But in some strange way the pain helped me—it took me out of the chaos of the put-in and made me focus on just moving past the injury and executing the dance routines. I couldn't concentrate on anything but getting past the pain of my throbbing knee. It was what I needed to get through the moment.

Opening night was a thrill. A culmination of a dream. All my friends from college were in the audience, plus my parents and family. The house was packed—it was standing-room only. I looked out at the audience and thought, *This is the night. This is what I do.* I said to myself, "I always knew that once the dust settled, I'd be on a Broadway stage!"

Chita had sent a note in the shape of a spider's web to my dressing room. "Welcome to the web!"

· · ·

## HELEN ON *KISS OF THE SPIDER WOMAN*

Vanessa was remarkable. Even though I didn't cry, it was one of the most emotional times of my life. I watched my daughter fulfill one of her life's goals and do it so incredibly well. It was amazing, wonderful, and very emotional for me and for Milton as well—although not as much for him. Milton always loved everything Vanessa did, but I'm a bit pickier. Even if she bombed, he'd make excuses for her. I don't. This was a very proud moment for me. A moment where you forget about all those little hiccups—at least momentarily.

One morning a few days after opening night, I was dropping my daughters off at summer camp in the Bell Middle School parking lot when a mom approached me.

"Did you see the love letter to you in *The New York Times?*"

It was nine in the morning. I was a mom with a baby and two little girls. I didn't read *The New York Times* that early! Actually, I never read reviews. I'm not a crazy, neurotic example of what people think actors are like. I don't read reviews, google myself, or read online gossip. But reviewed in *The New York Times?* I left the parking lot and booked it to the nearest newsstand to check it out. The review read, "Ever since it opened more than fourteen months ago, *Kiss of the Spider Woman* has been one of Broadway's most thrilling musicals. Now that Vanessa Williams has joined the cast, it is also the sexiest. Sleek, proud, and breathtakingly confident, the recording star has taken over the role of Aurora, the exotic film goddess who prowls men's dreams and inflames their imaginations. Whenever she's onstage, the temperature in the Broadhurst Theater shoots up about twenty degrees. The air-conditioning bills are going to be hell to pay, but the box office is bound to start jumping as word of her performance gets around. . . . Ms. Williams, making her Broadway debut, adds a dimension to the production that has been missing until now: She is an irresistibly alluring temptress."

This was one of the most wonderful moments of my career—to get a great review by *The New York Times* for a role in a Broadway show! And to have no mention of my beauty queen past! Ramon designed wooden fans with my picture on one side and the review on the other to include in my media kit. Mom framed the review for me along with a ticket from opening night and the Playbill—my *Kiss of the Spider Woman* montage.

With the new cast in place, *Kiss of the Spider Woman* was supposed to have a limited run of three months. But after we got reviewed by *The New York Times,* the box-office ticket sales went through the roof. I'd heard they skyrocketed by as much as $100,000 a week. It became the hottest ticket in town because it was almost considered a new show, despite the fact that it had been on Broadway for more than a year. People who'd already seen it were coming to our version. People who hadn't seen it were suddenly curious about it.

And with me in the lead, the play attracted a diverse crowd of younger theatergoers as well as a tremendous black audience.

I thought of Lee Gershwin's comments ten years earlier, when she said I was a whore who'd attract the wrong type of theatergoers.

*Well, look at me now, Lee. I'm filling the house every night!*

I loved that we were able to surprise people with our fresh take. I loved that people were shocked that I could actually dance and perform on Broadway—even though that's what I had been trained to do. The attitude had been "Oh, she's just a singer. She couldn't possibly act and dance." I loved that I'm this underrated talent

## A FEW OTHER THINGS ABOUT ME THAT MIGHT SURPRISE YOU

- I secretly listen to Howard Stern. I didn't start until my morning commute into the city from Chappaqua when I was rehearsing *Into the Woods*. I was tired of urban radio and I wanted something different. I turned on Howard and was surprised at how funny, objective, normal, and smart he is. I love the banter and I'd find myself laughing out loud in the car.

- I love Irish music. I listen to Irish radio every Saturday morning on WFUV, Fordham University's radio station. Irish music is soulful and I find the themes of hope and despair align to the African-American experience. One day I hope to go to Ireland and do a horseback-riding tour through the lush green countryside.

- I have always loved horses. When I was a little girl, I'd ask Santa for a pony. Every Christmas I'd wake up and look out the window to see if one was tied up on the front lawn. It never happened. As a mom, I watched my daughters take riding lessons and I thought, *I should be doing this, too*. I started taking jumping lessons and now I'm a strong enough rider to ride anywhere. Whenever I travel, I ride. It gives you a whole different perspective on the place you're visiting. I love galloping along a beach as fast as possible. It's exhilarating, freeing, and exciting. Riding a horse connects to that side of me—my free-spirited youth.

- My dad taught me to pray as a little girl. I still pray every day right before I go to bed. Sometimes, I'm not on my knees, but other times, I am. I say how I am thankful for my blessings; I ask for guidance and trust that the way will be shown to me.

- I love salsa dancing. If I could, I would do it every day.
- I do the *New York Times* crossword puzzle every morning (except Friday and Saturdays because it's too hard—Monday is always a breeze). I love the mind exercise and the routine. Plus I love learning new vocabulary words.
- I'm a dreamer and a dancer. When I close my eyes and listen to music, my first thought is always a dance. My true nature is as a dancer.

because it's almost like having a secret weapon. No one expects much from me.

So when I deliver: Wow!

*Kiss* became such a sensation—it was extended for three months and then another three months. It was a crazy, hectic time.

Onstage, I was an alluring temptress. I'd get reviews calling me hot, hot, hot. Then I'd go home after a show, walk into the house, and transform back into a mom who had to take care of ear infections, comfort a crying child, and breast-feed my nearly two-year-old son (I could not get him to stop!)—the most maternal act there is.

Being on Broadway was glamorous, but the reality was I'd come home and be Mommy. I was swinging it all—performing in eight shows a week on Broadway, finishing an album, and trying to be the best mom and wife I could be. But I hardly saw Ramon and wondered, *Where the hell is he?* I thought, *Okay, this is how it has to be right now. This craziness is only temporary. Once the show ends its run and I finish my album, we'll be able to get back on track.*

When I wasn't onstage performing, I was in the studio working on *The Sweetest Days*. I wanted to make something that was different from my other albums. I didn't want it to be a traditional R & B album. I wanted to create music that was like a journey, moving from sultry jazz to acoustical soul to Brazilian pop.

"Sister Moon" was a song written by Sting, who also sings backup on the track. It was a treat to work with him because I'd been a huge fan and had seen him perform with the Police at the Carrier Dome in Syracuse during their *Synchronicity* tour while I was in college.

Babyface, who was being managed by Ramon, wrote and produced two of the cuts for the album and had been inspired by *Kiss of the Spider Woman*. "Betcha Never" was Latin influenced and the mid-tempo "You Can't Run" sounded very tropical. I also sang a remake of the Patti Austin hit "You Don't Have to Say You're Sorry," as well as a song called "Ellamental," a tribute to Ella Fitzgerald. We recorded in the studio with lava lamps glowing, incense burning, and candles flickering. It was a very intimate yet laid-back atmosphere.

I'd never been so fulfilled professionally. It was coming together so well that I decided to celebrate by hosting a New Year's Eve party at Sardi's, a restaurant in the theater district. I invited my family and the entire cast and crew of *Kiss of the Spider Woman*, plus their spouses. We had had a grueling day with two shows, so we wanted to let loose, have fun, celebrate our success, and ring in the New Year together—just like family.

Ramon was at Madison Square Garden where Babyface, his client, was performing with Boyz II Men. It was the first leg of a nineteen-date national tour and a big deal because Babyface never toured. Ramon was busy, but I assumed that he'd eventually slip away to be with me so we could welcome in the New Year together, as we did every year since we'd been together. But he never showed up. He never called. He didn't come home that night.

It was my first New Year's alone, ever. I was surrounded by family, cast, and crew, but no husband. It was another tear in our already fraying relationship. This year I'd seen my dreams come true, yet here I was, celebrating the end of the year without my husband.

But the show must go on, right? I smiled, laughed, and counted down to the New Year with a roomful of joyous guests and hid the ache in my heart.

*Kiss of the Spider Woman* finally ended its run on my birthday, March 18, 1995. I was supposed to immediately go on tour stateside to promote *The Sweetest Days*. We had the band, choreographer, singers, and tour manager. We'd even started rehearsals. Then I got a call from my agent saying that a big-budget movie starring Arnold Schwarzenegger was being cast.

"You can't do this. Everything's ready to go," Ramon said.

"I need to do this."

Ramon was furious—all that work, all that time might be for naught. It was a battle over music and acting. Which, or in this case who, would win?

How could he expect me to pass up an action-adventure movie starring one of the hottest box-office stars? If I got the part, didn't he know how great this would be for my career?

It's what I wanted, and I had to speak up!

*Sometimes people will come up to me and ask, "Are you Vanessa Williams's mother?" I'm proud when her fans recognize me and I always answer, "Yes." But that's not my only accomplishment. Vanessa has a brother, Chris, who is also in show business. And I have an identity of my own. However, being "the mother" does offer many rewards. Yippee!*

—HELEN WILLIAMS

The story goes that Arnold Schwarzenegger was compiling a list of costars for *Eraser*, a big-budget action-adventure movie, when his then-wife, Maria Shriver, chimed in: "You know who I think would be great? Vanessa Williams."

"She doesn't act—she's a singer," he said.

Arnold only knew me as a recording artist. But Maria was persistent. "She's an actress, too, and she's great. At least have her audition."

Maria and I had met years earlier when she had interviewed me for NBC News shortly after the Miss America scandal. We had become instant friends—bonding over the fact that we both felt we had so much to prove. As a member of political royalty (Sargent and Eunice Kennedy Shriver were her parents, President John F. Kennedy her uncle), Maria always felt that people didn't take her seriously as a journalist. And I'd spent years and years striving to move beyond my beauty queen image. When you meet someone who has had similar struggles, friendships are easily forged.

It seemed Maria was the only one who believed I'd be perfect for the role of Lee Cullen, a senior executive at a weapons company who discovers corruption and is placed in a witness protection program. Arnold, whose character was a U.S. Marshal assigned to protect her, wasn't convinced.

Neither was Arnold Kopelson, the producer, who didn't consider me a feature-film actor; Chuck Russell, the director, wanted Madeleine Stowe.

And Ramon didn't want me to consider it.

"I can't believe you want to do this now," he said. "We have plans. You're rehearsing and we're supposed to go on tour. I already have all the dates lined up for you."

He'd worked so hard to get my tour together and I was just abandoning it. I knew this was an opportunity I just couldn't pass up. "I'm not canceling the tour," I told him. "I'm just postponing it."

But Ramon was faced with the stress of dealing with a looming lawsuit filed by the promoter in Japan for canceling all the tour dates, and we also had to settle on employment agreements with everyone who had signed up for the tour—all of whom wanted some compensation for the lost income they'd suffer as well as the "supposed" dates they had already given up and lost because they committed to touring with me. No one cared whether or not the tour would be rescheduled, and they all wanted something for their time.

This just led to more tension, more resentment, more pressure on the marriage.

As my husband, he should've understood. But as my manager he was furious. And I was angry that he was furious. At one time the manager-husband lines had been blurred. Now the lines weren't blurred; they'd been erased and husband Ramon had disappeared. All that remained was manager Ramon. I didn't want to be married to my manager. I wanted my husband back.

But where was he? He'd become so angry, so distant, so hard to reach.

I wanted this movie. I loved the idea of starring in a big-budget action-adventure with lots of explosions and chases. I flew myself out to Hollywood for a meeting with *Eraser's* producer and director. I had no idea that it was considered a big deal to fly out for a meeting on your dime. I didn't travel in showbiz circles. I just wanted this part and the producer and director didn't want to consider me. So I just booked a flight to change their mind. It made perfect sense to me. *I want the role. Here's the obstacle. Let me fix it.*

I met with the director and producer. Then I flew home to Chappaqua. A few days later, they flew me back to screen-test with Arnold. I knew I had to go in and kick ass. I had to prove I could act.

I met Arnold and he instantly put me at ease.

## HOW I MADE THE TERMINATOR CRY

In 2010 Maria Shriver asked me to sing at **Arnold Schwarzenegger's** holiday party at a Sacramento gala dinner shortly before he finished his term as governor of California. I wanted to do a parody of *The Sound of Music* song "So Long, Farewell." (So long, farewell, auf Wiedersehen, adieu—I think it's time to make *Eraser 2.*) But I also wanted to do another, more touching number. I called Maria and asked for her suggestions. The event was a week before Christmas and she told me that "Silent Night" was Arnold's very favorite song. Then a friend suggested, "Why don't you sing it in German?" Bingo! I had the song written phonetically on cards. As I was singing it, I looked over and Arnold's eyes were watering up. He couldn't believe I was singing it in German. Afterward, Maria said to me, "I've been married to him for more than twenty years and I can't make him cry."

"You know, you're a lot like me," he said. "People discounted us based on the way we looked. I was Mr. Universe. You were Miss America. But here we are—because of our strengths and courage. We showed them what we were made of."

The screen test went well. Kopelson asked me to lose ten pounds and I did. They gave me the part and then reworked the ending so we could distance ourselves from *The Bodyguard*, which had just been a huge hit. The movie, starring Whitney Houston and Kevin Costner, was about a black woman in distress and the white man who saves her. The studio was worried that if they hired me—a black woman and a singer—*Eraser* would look like another copycat movie (even though the part hadn't been written specifically for a black woman or a singer). So instead of falling in love, like Whitney and Kevin do, Arnold and I have a platonic relationship in the movie.

The film started shooting in New York in August 1995 and wrapped in Los Angeles in April 1996—nearly twice as long as we had expected. Working with Arnold was always an adventure. He was always in charge. He was forever saying, "Very nice." It was his catchphrase after a job well-done. People paid attention each time he arrived on set and he was always a complete gentleman.

At his fiftieth birthday party, Gina Gershon and I sang "Happy Birthday," Marilyn Monroe–style (and we presented him with a rocking chair).

During the filming, my children were in school in Chappaqua, so I was constantly on planes going back and forth. Ramon was busy working with Babyface, so he was constantly on the road, too. I flew back nearly every weekend. All the money I made went to pay for my plane tickets. I'd get off the red-eye and go back to being Mom—driving the kids to gymnastics, karate, and birthday parties, or suiting them up in their Rollerblades, helmets, and wrist guards.

My parents pitched in. Our nanny, Kathi, helped, too. I wasn't going to let distance deter me from being there for my kids and my normal "non-Hollywood" life in the suburbs.

# CHAPTER
# 18

I was at school in between classes when Vanessa called with news I hadn't expected—she and Ramon were getting divorced.

She spoke in between sobs. "Could you come over?"

"Of course," I said.

I left school right away and headed to her place.

By the time I got there, Vanessa had calmed down. She was on the phone, talking to her business people while sorting through papers. She was figuring out what she needed to do to proceed with a divorce. She was dealing with it, not collapsing on her bed in tears. That's how we're similar. We don't wallow in self-pity.

Despite my early reservations, I had thought Ramon and Vanessa were a good couple. They both loved their family. Ramon had turned out to be an excellent father who always was involved in his children's lives. I don't know what their marriage was really like. Does anyone other than the couple involved really know why a marriage doesn't work? I think Vanessa spent a lot of years putting up a good front, but she had been unhappy for some time.

It sounds cliché, but they had really just grown apart. It was a struggle because they were both so completely involved in Vanessa's career. It ate up all their time and attention, and the marriage became a neglected child. Perhaps if they had seen this and had hired someone else to be Vanessa's manager, they'd still be together.

There had been tension between them and they were arguing a lot. I know that was something that really bothered Vanessa—a home filled with stress. She had been raised in a very calm household and she wanted that for her children. Even though the kids were very young, they knew something was wrong. Vanessa and Ramon knew it was better to get divorced than to subject their children to their problems.

Vanessa and Ramon handled it well. They wanted what was best for the children. They put their differences aside so that the kids would have two parents showing up for their sports games and dance recitals. Even though they were no longer together as a married couple, their decision to remain committed to each other as parents is commendable. Some people don't even realize they're divorced.

*Ramon and me on the beach—our life in the L.A. sun*

# PART FOUR

# TODAY
## AND EVERYDAY

*I try not to offer Vanessa advice unless asked. Then
I will freely give my honest opinion with constructive
suggestions. Otherwise, I listen and support. I act as a
sounding board when Vanessa is trying to work through
a situation. And usually she resolves it on her own.*

—HELEN WILLIAMS

Wow, you look fabulous," friends would tell me. "What's your secret?"

"Misery." I'm skinniest when I'm miserable. I can't eat because my stomach is in knots, and I lose twenty pounds in two weeks. Breakups and deaths do wonders for my body—but who wants to lose weight that way? After Ramon and I separated, it was a relief. I had spent a long time being sad, angry, and full of resentment. Secretly, I was also terrified—I'd never been without a man in my adult life. Actually, ever since I was sixteen, I was in a relationship. I was thirty-three years old and single for the first time ever.

I never imagined that I'd be divorced. It just wasn't something I considered a possibility. When I said my vows at the altar at St. Francis Xavier, I meant them. I took "till death do you part" very seriously. My parents had set a gold standard that I assumed I'd follow. I wanted what they had—the stability, the friendship, and the deep, mutual love and respect. But the tension between Ramon and me became something we could no longer live with. Marriage counseling, confession, even a new location to start over didn't solve our issues.

Did I blame Ramon? Of course I did, at first. I had felt so abandoned. I felt he had checked out of our marriage a long time ago. We lived parallel lives. But time has made me reconsider. Now I can say I blame *us*. Maybe we didn't work hard enough on our marriage. Maybe I spent so much time on my career and my children that I neglected him. Maybe he liked being my hero, my rescuer, and then when my career finally took off, our roles changed. I had transformed over the years—I was no longer the twentysomething girl who was afraid to speak her mind and who counted on Ramon for all the answers. I was a confident woman who didn't want to take all of Ramon's advice, who didn't follow all of his suggestions. I think he felt betrayed by the new me. I had come into my own and this somehow rendered him less important—at least in his eyes.

I had become much more forthright in my feelings and opinions. I've discovered that many women marry men for their potential and pray they live up to the expectations, whereas men marry women hoping they'll never change and have issues when they do transform and grow. Let's hope I've learned to accept what I have and live in the present and be grateful.

I was lucky that my parents lived so close to me. They'd pick up the children from school, drive them to their sports and dance lessons, help with their homework, read to them, and teach them piano. Mom was always looking for fun activities to keep the kids' minds off the divorce. Whenever there were concerts, fall festivals, or plays, Mom would pack the kids in the car and go. Dad was really big on tradition and consistency—he took the kids to local parades,

Easter egg hunts, and to see Fourth of July fireworks. Every year he'd drive them to a farm upstate where they'd cut down our Christmas tree and then stop at Grandma's, a restaurant and pie shop in Yorktown, on the way back home, a Christmas tree strapped on top of the car.

Whenever I've faced a huge obstacle or passage in my life, I've never felt alone. I've always been surrounded by love and family. In my life, it really does take a village.

My dad hated divorce. It was hard for Dad to accept that my marriage had ended. He was a big proponent of keeping marriages together. He believed that there was no problem that couldn't be worked out if you had patience and commitment. When I first told him I was getting divorced, he'd said to me, "Don't make any rash decisions." He had counseled other family members through rocky times in their marriages, and Dad thought he could help Ramon and me.

Mom would always stick up for me and say, "Oh, Milton, can't you see she's done? She's had enough."

The divorce was hard on all the kids, but especially Melanie, the oldest, who was nine. She was angry and confused. Sometimes she'd lash out at me; other times it was at Ramon. She'd burst into tears and retreat to her room.

But Ramon and I had made a pact to put the children first. We had to get past our resentments and establish some sort of friendship. We didn't have any bitter feuds over property or custody. (I got the house, with all its debt from the renovations.) We both wanted to be there for all the major milestones in our children's lives— birthday parties, dance recitals, sporting events, First Communions, graduations. And we definitely didn't want to be the parents of the stressed-out kids who had to worry that their mom and dad would kill each other if they were in the same room. We continued to attend mass together on Sundays at Saint John and Saint Mary, our parish church (we still do when the kids are all home). Ramon and I wanted to set an example for the children. We were together so much that some of the kids' friends didn't even realize we were divorced.

Ramon moved nearby and we split custody during the week. I had Monday and Tuesday; Ramon had Wednesday and Thursday. Then we switched off every other weekend. We made it work. Ramon always lived only five minutes away. The only real inconvenience was that the kids would leave books, clothes, or favorite stuffed animals at one home, when they wanted them at the other home. We were constantly driving back and forth to retrieve forgotten items.

It was tough on all of us. Divorce is the most painful experience, especially when there are kids involved. But I felt that Ramon really stepped up and became an even better, more involved father as a result of being divorced. I have seen so many friends who go through wicked divorces and the kids wind up being the pawns in the parents' head games. Kids suffer enough during a divorce—it's just not fair to put them in the middle of their parents' issues. The only time it would get weird and uncomfortable was when we had "others." At the girls' first dance recital after our split, Ramon showed up with a new girlfriend on his arm. The whispers started: "Who's that?" But "Team V" was there to support me. Women want to protect and unite. I guess that's what friends are for.

I never knew how quiet a house could be until the kids weren't with me. It took a long time for me to adjust to the silence. My first Christmas alone really crushed me. I'm such a big lover of traditions, especially at the holidays. I love having the family all together.

That year, 1996, Christmas seemed so quiet without my kids, who were in Los Angeles with Ramon's family for our first Christmas as separate parents. I stared at the decorated tree at our rental on Paulding Drive (the home renovations weren't complete yet). As hard as I tried to stay positive, I couldn't help but feel a bit depressed. I thought about our rituals—Christmas Eve mass at five fifteen, followed by a big homemade lasagna dinner back at my house. Afterward, the kids would run over to the tree, where they were allowed to open one of their presents.

At the time I had a new love—a handsome and talented writer-director who I'd met on location in Turkey while filming *The Odyssey*. We went to mass together, but I couldn't stop thinking about my children and wondering what they were doing in Los Angeles with their dad. We watched the Christmas Eve pageant and I missed my children even more as I listened to the voices of their classmates singing Christmas carols with the choir.

I started writing in a journal. I have stacks of journals—from high school until now. When I was younger, I wrote everything in them all the time. But as I got older, I'd only write when I was distressed. It is my way to check in on my emotions. It helps with grieving. It helps with forgiving. Sometimes when I write down my thoughts, I can feel the stress, the anger, and the resentment leave my body and settle on the pages where they stay.

My mother understood what a difficult time this was for me in a way I didn't expect. She and my dad had such a strong marriage that I didn't think she could relate to the pain I was experiencing. But I realized that because she had such a lonely childhood, she knew what it was like to feel alone and abandoned.

She also understood me better than I realized. She knew how much I hated failing, and I felt like I'd failed in my marriage. One day before I had gotten divorced, Mom handed me a book called *The Value in the Valley* by Iyanla Vanzant, an inspirational speaker, an ordained minister, and a frequent guest on *Oprah*. The book's message is that life is not just a series of peaks or mountaintop experiences but often a difficult journey through dark valleys. I devoured it and reread it during the difficult times.

I definitely felt that I was in a dark valley, but I would get out of it by focusing on my family and my career. I also knew that I would get beyond my resentment. That's how I'm different from my mom. I process things quickly, whereas Mom will stay angry for a while. She'll hold on to everything and remember any little insult—that's why once you're on her "List" you can never come off. I can't live like that.

Through all this marital upheaval, I was also in the midst of renovating my Chappaqua home, a project Ramon and I had started together in the fall of 1995. When we'd bought the house, I'd fallen in love with the 1905 stone-and-glass contemporary, the renovated carriage house as well as the five acres of property, especially the duck pond in front. But we wanted to double the size of the house to eight thousand square feet. We wanted to add two bedrooms so the girls could have their own rooms. We wanted to build a big master bathroom and a formal dining room. I wanted to create an atmosphere that would have the feel of a relaxed, airy seaside cottage—the type of home you see straddling the shoreline in Nantucket or Martha's Vineyard.

In my Filofax (back in the day when people kept information on pages instead of on BlackBerrys and iPhones), I wrote a list of all the things I wanted in my dream home: a long driveway perched on a hill, lots of stone and glass, plenty of sunlight, a few fireplaces, a pond, a pool, a tennis court.

But this home-renovations project had turned into a money pit. What we had thought would take a year was now nearing two years with no end in sight. The renovations were supposed to cost $700,000 in total, but I'd already gone well over the million-dollar mark. I fired the architect and the contractor took over. I'd set up a timetable with the contractor—but every change pushed the end date. My savings were being depleted. I was always writing a check for one thing or another. At times I felt like I was being bamboozled and not being heard. I was rolling with the big boys in terms of contracting, and I didn't know what I was doing.

The children and I moved from one rental home to the next. We had even lived at my parents' house, where I slept in my brother's bunk bed! Wasn't I a star of the stage, screen, and radio? And here I was, huddled in Chris's room with New York Yankees and Georgetown Hoyas memorabilia pinned to the walls.

I couldn't oversee the project every day because I had to work to pay for the project. I was starring in back-to-back-to-back-*to-back* movies—*Hoodlum, Soul Food, Dance with Me,* and *The Odyssey.* I'd be gone for weeks and return home to be disappointed with the progress. The house was in shambles. I had a specific vision—I wanted a home that felt open and spacious with high-beamed ceilings and a lot of angles.

"I don't want curved walls." Another redo.

"I don't want a stone wall that looks like a fortress." More money.

I was not in control of the project and I needed help.

The contractor would insist that everything be done in the proper way. There was always an answer and an explanation. This was my first time doing a home renovation and I was all alone.

So I asked my dad to step in and be the checks-and-balances guy. It seemed like a perfect idea since he loved construction. He knew a lot about building, so I could count on him to supervise and get these guys back on track.

Dad being Dad—the most likeable person I know—quickly became friends with the Croatian construction crew. They had already moved into my home and were sleeping downstairs in the playroom. The contractor even turned the living room into his makeshift office, complete with a desk filled with all his plans and diagrams. It was so homey that one warm day the crew threw a big lamb roast in the family-room addition to give us a taste of Croatian tradition. Everyone was getting along great.

But I still had no home to move into!

More time passed. I was in Chicago shooting *Hoodlum*, a period gangster movie starring Laurence Fishburne. Everything was on schedule, the contractor assured me.

When I returned from Chicago, I drove to the house and was shocked.

There was stone everywhere! Obviously I hadn't read the plans correctly. I wanted relaxed and elegant, but my grounds looked like a medieval fortress! The contractor was so proud of his work. It was beautifully done, but the contractor's aesthetic was so different from mine. I wanted light, airy, and rustic, and I was getting solid, massive, and medieval. And that was the outside. I had already gone through two interior designers, each not seeing my vision of relaxed, substantial "California country."

On my next visit to Los Angeles, I checked into my favorite hotel, Shutters on the Beach in Santa Monica, and it hit me: This is the feeling I want! It had that open, airy, beach-cottage vibe I wanted for my home. As I checked in, I asked the concierge, "Who designed this place?"

Mark Enos and his firm, they told me.

Finally! I didn't have to explain anymore!

I called Mark.

"Listen, my home is in shambles. I want what you did to Shutters. I want the floors, the ceilings, the fireplace. I want the entire look. Basically, I want Shutters to be my home."

I flew him and his designer/partner, Lynne Miyake, to Chappaqua. They walked around the house, took some notes, and said, "We get it."

Mark and his team worked with the contractor and started making a lot of changes. But the contractor was still not meeting deadlines. I was spending more and more money. The situation felt as stressful as the divorce I had just gone through.

I had to make another tough decision. I needed a new contractor to implement Mark and Lynne's vision. So right before Thanksgiving 1997, after two years of not living in my home, I fired Joe, the contractor, and his team.

My father was livid. These were great men and talented craftsmen. He felt they deserved to finish the project. But I had already spent more than $1.8 million and my house was unlivable.

Dad knew I was frustrated and tired of not having a home. But he was overseeing the project and I hadn't consulted him. In Dad's eyes, I had betrayed him. In Dad's eyes, I didn't need him anymore.

Dad was so disappointed in my decision that he stopped talking to me. As it turned out, I had to spend another $800,000 tearing down the work to restore my vision—changing stone to wood and curved walls to straight ones. Basically we had to start from scratch. Dad would have to understand that I was going to end up with everything I wanted. I was not going to compromise.

At Thanksgiving that year we had dinner at Gaga's and Papa's (my folks) in Millwood. When I was a kid, we'd head to my grandmother's in Buffalo. Now, we alternate—sometimes Mom hosts it,

## MOM'S MOST DELICIOUS MEALS
### (ACCORDING TO VANESSA)

- Roast chicken
- Baked beans with sausage
- Apple pie (from scratch)
- Tomato sandwiches on toast (fresh from our garden outside)

## VANESSA'S MOST DELICIOUS MEALS
### (ACCORDING TO HELEN)

- Lemon squares
- Yogurt berry pie
- Thanksgiving turkey (She's taken over the tradition in recent years and she makes a delicious turkey. She soaks it in brine and stuffs the cavity with oranges and lemons. Of course, she only buys organic. I, on the other hand, used to buy whatever the A&P had on sale.)

sometimes I do. If it's at Mom's, she'll cook the turkey and the candied sweet potatoes. Dad would always make mashed potatoes and a delicious cranberry relish with liquor and nuts. Dad was the baker in the family and he'd make wonderful breads and muffins. I'd bring over some sides like macaroni and cheese (with Gouda instead of cheddar).

I thought my father and I could get past our disagreement and enjoy the holiday, but when I walked into the house I could tell that wouldn't be the case. Usually Dad greeted me with a great big bear hug and a "Happy Thanksgiving, Ness!" But he didn't come to the door. When I walked in the house, he ignored me. He didn't speak during the meal, except to ask someone to pass the turkey. He didn't address me at all. It was unbearable. I knew my father was upset, but that Thanksgiving it became clear how enraged he was.

At the beginning of the Thanksgiving meal, we have a family tradition. We go around the table and each person has to say something he or she is thankful for. My dad would usually lead it. He would be thankful for everything—his wife, his children, his grand-children.

When it was his turn to speak, Dad looked down at the table and said, "Pass."

What? My father was too furious to be thankful!

After an extremely tense dinner, I went into the kitchen to clean the dishes and slammed them against the counter, thinking I'd get some sort of reaction from Dad. He'd get angry, we'd have a confrontation, and then we'd get over it. But Dad just ignored me—and if you really want to drive me crazy, that's how to do it. I hate being ignored. Doesn't everyone?

I went back home to my latest rental and I didn't feel very thankful, either. My dad has always been my hero, my confidant, the person I called for advice or just to vent. Now he was disappointed with me again. It killed me. He stopped coming over to the house to give the kids music lessons. He stopped dropping off firewood.

My mom became the go-between, which was a new position for her. I don't hold grudges. Family comes first. Perhaps after a few days, we'd all calm down. He'd be back to teach the kids piano, or he'd answer my call when I asked for some type of advice. Either way, we'd be back in each other's lives soon, as if nothing had ever happened.

I didn't know on that Thanksgiving evening that my dad and I wouldn't talk again for more than a year, or that our disagreement would never truly be resolved. Instead of confronting the issues as we'd done during the family meetings of my childhood, we left it to simmer.

I finally moved to my home the following June of 1998. My father didn't come to see the finished project for months and months. When he finally took the tour, he said nothing, even though I was so proud to have the house I always wanted.

## HELEN ON THANKSGIVING

When Milton found out that Vanessa had fired the crew, he was livid. I hadn't seen him that angry in a long, long time— since the Bruce days. Milton had such strong feelings about other people's feelings. He couldn't wrap his head around Vanessa's firing the crew. He thought they were such nice, talented guys. He appreciated anyone who was creative and took pride in their work. His projects were always done to perfection. He would settle for nothing less and he admired this trait in others. But what I think really upset him was the manner in which Vanessa fired the crew: Marshals came to escort them off the property. I'm not sure who advised her to take that action, but in her father's eyes it was bad advice and was unacceptable behavior on Vanessa's part. I could understand that Vanessa wasn't happy with the results and needed to do something about it, but Milton didn't see it that way. For him to say "Pass" on Thanksgiving was a huge deal. I knew he was just so upset that he could barely speak. He was too upset to talk about it with me. Vanessa was crushed. I was in the middle of it and feeling very stressed. More turkey, anyone?

The next time I touched my dad was on September 26, 1999, when I slipped my arm under his as he walked me down the aisle of the Church of the Holy Trinity to marry Rick Fox. At the reception, we danced to the Jackson 5's *ABC* with big smiles on our faces, surrounded by a gang of elegantly dressed kids.

There was no distinct olive branch offered or conversation to address the issue. Dad started teaching Devin the sax and came over to the new house to give lessons, bring firewood for my pile, and help with advice on oil burners, AC units, and additional projects.

I recently spoke at a Catholic girls' school in Manhattan. After the talk (about overcoming obstacles), a young girl approached me.

"My dad built your house," she said.

I told the girl to say hi to her dad for me. I also told her to tell her father that my father had died. Later that week, I received a lovely note from him saying how sorry he was to hear about my dad's sudden passing. "Your dad was a great man," Joe wrote.

# CHAPTER
## 20

*Vanessa's man is out there somewhere—she just hasn't found him yet. Or she doesn't recognize him yet. But one of these days, she will. Or I will—and I'll have to give her a nudge!*

—HELEN WILLIAMS

It is hard for me to date. I have had serious relationships since I was sixteen. I was with Joe for a year, Bruce for four years, and then I was with Ramon for twelve years and ten months. I love being with a partner and in a committed relationship.

I don't get asked out on dates that much. Actually it rarely happens. People just assume that I'm leading this really glamorous life and dating all these handsome, interesting men, but usually I'm working or at home with the kids. When I do venture out, it's with my girlfriends or my gay friends or even my priest friend. I tease Father Edward, "When I asked God for the perfect man, I should have been more specific!"

But I love being in a serious relationship. I love taking care of someone and having someone take care of me—sharing meals, sharing stories, sharing dreams. I love being desired and feeling

connected to someone. My mom would say I'm a hopeless romantic. What's wrong with that?

The summer after Ramon and I separated, I was cast as Calypso
in *The Odyssey*, an NBC miniseries starring Armand Assante, Greta
Scacchi, and Isabella Rossellini. The shoot was in Ölüdeniz, a beautiful resort village on the Aegean Sea in Turkey.

It was my first time away as a single woman. The kids stayed for
the first week of rehearsals and sightseeing. Then when it was time
to shoot, they headed back to New York with Kathi.

Once we started shooting, our day would end at sundown. I'd
head downstairs to the bar with Kate Best, my makeup pal, and
Oscar James, my hair buddy. We'd order drinks and eat hot cheese.
I felt young again—not like a mother of three.

Chris Solimine, who wrote the teleplay, was a confident, dark,
and handsome Italian guy from Westfield, New Jersey, who loved
Irish pubs, the Yankees, and a good argument. He had come up to
me at the welcome party and asked if the kids and I needed a drink.
He says I blew him off, but I was in "mommy" mode. The celebrity
thing can be intimidating to men, but Chris scored big points with
me right away because he just came right on up.

Chris mentioned he went to Syracuse University at the same
time I did. We were even in the same year but didn't know each
other. I was down at the theater at Syracuse Stage Complex—he
was up on the hill, where the main campus was located. We instantly hit it off because of our shared past. We got each other's
jokes and references. It was comfortable as well as hot and heavy.
He became my first as a single woman.

We watched classic movies together. He traveled with me on the
road when I toured with Luther Vandross (he was my band's favorite boyfriend; they still ask about him). He gave great notes while I
was shooting *Soul Food* in Chicago. He became a love of my life.
Chris was deep, sensitive, joyful, and complex.

We were together when I moved back into my home. Although

he loved my newly renovated house, he sighed, "I could never give you this." But I didn't want that from him. I already had the house. I just wanted him. That was enough.

We were together for two years—from Turkey to Chicago to Malibu to New York to a tour bus—filled with excitement, passion, and frustration. I don't know why we were constantly breaking up and getting back together.

One afternoon, Chris, an avid movie enthusiast, had taken me to see Spike Lee's *He Got Game*. Little did we know that nearly a year later, I would wind up marrying one of its stars, Rick Fox. (My first image of him was in a hot tub surrounded by naked blondes—an image that would come to haunt me.)

"There's this guy—a forward—for the Lakers who is gorgeous and you'd make a beautiful couple," said Lynne, my interior designer, when she was working on the house. Lynne was a huge Los Angeles Lakers fan and was obsessed with this new team member.

"What? I've got Chris. I'm not interested in some guy from the Lakers," I told her. "Plus, I'm a Knicks fan, and I don't date athletes."

Lynne smiled knowingly. "You haven't seen him yet."

That February, I was invited to a book signing for my dear friend Sam Fine, a celebrity makeup artist. I was so proud of Sam—he was blowing up. So Chris and I went and we took Lynne along since she was in town helping with the house. We were seated in a booth upstairs in the VIP area. Ramon was there, too—downstairs at the bar. Isaiah Thomas sat with us, and Chris and Lynne were all over him since they were huge fans. I'd met Isaiah when he and Magic Johnson had seen me years ago in *One Man Band* off-Broadway.

Tyra Banks crossed into the VIP section followed by a huge hunk of a man. We said our usual "Hey, girl." Then she introduced this hunk to our table.

"Nice to meet you," he said politely.

Our eyes locked for a quick second and Lynne kicked me under the table. When he left, she blurted out: "That's who I was talking about. That's Rick Fox."

*Oooh, now I get it. He's gorgeous.*

Rick had been in New York for the all-star game, but was heading back to Los Angeles.

*When's my next trip to L.A?* I wondered, as Chris sat next to me and Ramon was downstairs at the bar.

Past, present, and future all at the same time at a New York City spot called Metronome.

Five months later I made it to Los Angeles for the press junket and premiere of *Dance with Me*, the ballroom dance movie I starred in with Chayanne, the Puerto Rican mega–pop singer and total hunk. Chris didn't want to come out for the premiere.

Lynne, who lived in Los Angeles, called and said, "There's a birthday party for Rick Fox at Century Club? Want to go?"

A: I don't know him. B: I'm going salsa dancing with my girls. C: I don't crash birthday parties.

*Or do I?*

Gena Avery, my assistant, got the address of the club and we pulled up in our rental. I chickened out. "Let's just drive around the block and then go in for a minute," Gena said.

"Okay, we'll go in for a minute," I agreed. After all, Chris and I were taking a break, even though I didn't want to.

Rick's twenty-ninth birthday party was packed with friends, family, and fans. Gena and I were ushered through by security to Rick. He was so happy we made it. He gave us each a glass of champagne and we toasted his birthday. He introduced me to his sisters, Jeanene and Sarah, and his brother, Aaron. His family was stunning. Then Gena and I began to head out to go salsa dancing.

"If you want to come to my premiere tomorrow, Gena will arrange a ticket for you," I told Rick on the way to the door.

"Sure, I'd love that."

Gena and I left, headed to El Floridita, and danced. Salsa dancing is really my favorite way to spend an evening. When the dancing is good, I'm completely drenched in sweat. It's the best workout in the world. Whenever we traveled for a movie or a tour, Gena would always go online and do some research and find the hottest salsa club in whatever city, town, or village. We'd show up and scout out the best dancers. It's not about finding the hottest guy. It's about looking for the best dancer who will give you the best workout—the guy who knows what he's doing.

Liz Curtis, who trained me for *Dance with Me*, was an eleven-time World Latin champ, but it was her sizzle on the salsa floor that fascinated me about this redhead from outside Boston. I met Liz during my run in *Kiss of the Spider Woman*. Her husband, Colton, joined me onstage as an inmate eight times a week, and Liz and Colton would salsa dance at cast parties. I would marvel at the ease, fluidity, and sensuality she brought to the dance floor.

So I couldn't wait to learn a new form of ballroom and Latin dance when I was cast as the female lead in *Dance with Me* after Sandra Bullock pulled out. And I got the offer. Liz Curtis had watched me dancing onstage on Broadway, so she knew I could learn the choreography of a ballroom instructor.

While training for the film, we would go to the clubs at night to practice the moves and combinations I was learning in the studio during the day. I was hooked and still am to this day.

Rick showed up late for the *Dance with Me* premiere, but stayed for the after-party and saw me in my glory—dancing all night and being passed around from dancer to dancer. I spun and twirled so much I'm surprised I didn't get a headache. I saw Rick from across the floor as I caught my breath in between dances and I thanked him for coming.

The next day I walked into my hotel room—there were three dozen pink and white roses.

I opened the note.

*Thanks for inviting me to the premiere. —Rick.*

That was nice, but off to New York I went.

I didn't need another relationship. He was handsome, but I needed some "me" time. Besides, I had told myself years ago that I'd never ever date a professional athlete. They were nothing but trouble. And Rick was six years younger than I was. Did I really want to be that woman with the younger man?

As luck would have it, Rick was filming a movie in New York (*Resurrection*) during the NBA lockout that ran into the 1998–1999 season. Rick was calling, Chris was wavering, and I was cautiously open.

I was in New York. Rick was in New York. There was time to date.

I got the full-court press from Rick. We went to dinner. He met my kids when he came to Chappaqua. He was unrelenting. A blind item ran in the local press after we were seen eating at a restaurant across from the Metropolitan Museum of Art.

*"Former beauty queen dines with pro NBA player formerly from UNC."*

It was thrilling and in some ways it was an escape—I was thirty-five years old, divorced, and a mom with three kids. Rick reminded me that I could still be young. Rick was twenty-nine and had never been married.

Halloween, Thanksgiving, and Christmas were all spent together at my house. In some ways, it was almost too perfect; everyone seemed to get along really well—the children and the adults. Ramon, who was raised in Los Angeles, was a fan of the Lakers. That was easy—a pro athlete from his favorite team available for basketball discussion. And they seemed to genuinely like each other. It was a really smooth transition. Ramon was happy I'd found someone who made me happy. Devin and Kyle, Rick's son from a previous relationship, hit it off immediately and soon became like brothers.

And Mom?

Believe it or not, she seemed to really like the idea of Rick . . . at first.

But I wasn't going to get serious. Once the lockout ended, Rick would head back to Los Angeles, where he'd have to remain for nine months of the year. That was no way to have a relationship. And there was no way I would be moving my family back to Los Angeles! The kids had had enough transition in their young lives.

In November, Rick whisked me away to his hometown of Nassau in the Bahamas for the weekend, and I could feel myself relaxing and letting my guard down. We romped in our room, took long walks on the beach, and ate delicious meals. I met his recently divorced parents. Rick and I shared stories, went deep-sea fishing. I told him how painful it was to be estranged from my dad. Rick understood that not being close to my dad was hell for me. He suggested I write my dad a letter. I took his advice.

By the end of the weekend, I thought to myself, *This feels good*.

*Heading to sound check in the back of the limo with Chris*

*In the midst of the rumba with Rick Valenzuela for a* DANCE WITH ME *competition scene*

# CHAPTER

# 21

I rang Vanessa's doorbell to let her know I was visiting. Then I just let myself in and walked up her circular staircase and into the living room. There, sitting on a couch, looking very comfortable—actually, too comfortable—was this enormous man. It was about nine at night, so I knew this wasn't some guy stopping by to bring her a delivery. This was some guy who'd spent time at Vanessa's house before and, for whatever reason, Vanessa had chosen not to mention him to me.

Vanessa was doing something in the kitchen and she very casually—too casually—said, "Oh, Mom, this is Rick. Rick Fox."

Vanessa said it in a way that implied he was someone famous, but I'd never heard of Rick Fox. Why would I? Milton and I never followed sports. Then Rick stood up.

Wow! He was even bigger than I thought. He's six foot seven. I think I uttered, "Oh my God."

Why is he at Vanessa's house looking like he belonged? Oh no, here we go again.

Rick treated her well and really tried to woo all of us. And believe me, I'm not one to be easily wooed. I'm always thinking, *What's this about? Why is he trying so hard?* For Mother's Day he sent me an enormous bouquet of flowers. When we stayed at an Atlantic City hotel where Vanessa was performing, he ordered in platters and platters of food for everybody.

Vanessa is really, *really* a romantic. I can't stress that enough. She loved that he would just take her away for a weekend. Because he wasn't playing basketball, all he did was concentrate on pursuing Vanessa. That became his job. It felt new and special to Vanessa, but I don't think she knew what he was really like as a person. It was like a vacation for him while his real life was on hold.

Looking back, I feel like Vanessa represented a huge challenge for him. He had a thing for her while he was growing up and, it seemed, as a sports star he was then able to set his sights on her. I've heard how some of these professional athletes can be when pursuing women. I'm wondering if he just said, "I'm going to get her." And then he did everything to make sure he did.

Maybe I'm wrong, but as you've probably figured out . . .

I'm usually not.

# CHAPTER
## 22

*Even if you have an in with the producer, you can still wind up on the cutting room floor.*

—HELEN WILLIAMS

I peed on a stick while playing a nun and prayed that I wasn't pregnant.

I was in Montreal, starring in the Lifetime television movie *The Courage to Love*, the true-life story of Mother Henriette Delille. Henriette, a black woman from a multiracial background, eschewed the pre–Civil War tradition of the "Quadroon Ball," an annual affair in New Orleans where wealthy French and Spanish men would choose racially mixed women to be their concubines. Instead, Henriette became a nun, opting for a life of poverty over privilege. She founded the first African-American order of nuns in the 1800s and became the first woman of African-American descent in the United States to have her cause for canonization recognized by the Roman Catholic Church.

A story of a black woman who performed miracles—I need to bring this to life!

I love faith-based movies and I love movies with strong female protagonists, so I signed on to produce—my first producing gig—and star in it. Emily Gerson-Saines, my former agent, who'd become my manager, helped produce the project in record time. I brought in my brother, Chris, who is also an actor, to play the master of ceremonies in a ballroom scene. My mother was an extra in the movie, and all the kids had cameos. It was a family affair—minus my dad, who still wasn't speaking to me.

During the shoot, Rick had flown in from Los Angeles to surprise me for the weekend. We hadn't been able to see much of each other because our schedules were so hectic. So, well, let's just say we had a lot of catching up to do.

When it came to birth control, I was practicing the rhythm method. You keep track of your cycle and calculate when you're fertile and when you're not. Plus, there's also a great deal of trust involved. "Didn't you pull out?" "You said you pulled out!" Yes, I've uttered those words before.

So when Rick visited, I thought I was safe the first night. And the rest of the visit, I knew we had to be careful. But travel, stress, and sleep changes can throw off your cycle.

Rick and I thought we had been careful. We enjoyed our hot August rendezvous in Montreal. He left to get ready for the season and I headed back to the movie.

A few weeks later, I was running on the treadmill at the hotel gym. I had a few more days left in Montreal and I started to think about what was next. In a couple of days, I'd perform in Dallas with the Dallas Symphony Orchestra and Yo-Yo Ma. Then I was back in New York to star in a remake of *Shaft* with Samuel L. Jackson. But the most exciting was I'd be on Broadway, starring as Queenie in *The Wild Party,* directed by George C. Wolfe. I had originated the part during the workshop at the Public Theater along with Mandy Patinkin, Eartha Kitt, and Keith David. Scott Rudin, a big-time movie producer, was taking us to Broadway after he produced *Shaft*. This was my dream—to originate a role on Broadway.

As I was running, I thought, *When was my last period?*

I didn't have any symptoms at all. I just realized I hadn't gotten my period when I was supposed to. I was just a few days late. But I was always like clockwork.

I asked Gena to get me a pregnancy test.

## MY MOST IMPORTANT CALLS TO MOM

- As a sophomore at Horace Greeley High School, I landed the lead role—Countess Aurelia (the Madwoman of Chaillot)—in the musical *Dear World*. It was a huge deal for a sophomore to land the lead, so the first call was to my mom because I knew she'd be thrilled. I think she was more excited than I was.
- When I won Miss Syracuse, I called Mom, who said, "That's terrific! How much money did you get?"
- When I was nominated for my first Grammy as Best New Artist for *The Right Stuff*, my first call was to Mom.
- When I learned that I was pregnant with Sasha and decided to get married to Rick, I called Mom to tell her that I was coming to her hotel room with some news. I think she had no idea what I was going to tell her when I arrived.

I peed on the stick, thinking how bizarre this was. Here I am, a divorced woman who may be pregnant and I'm playing a Catholic nun. This is not the time.

But guess what? I was pregnant.

As soon as I calmed down, I took a deep breath and called Rick. Would he be freaked out? Angry? Happy? I wasn't sure.

Rick answered the phone and I just blurted it out.

"You're not going to believe this. Remember your visit? I'm pregnant."

"WHAT?"

"You heard me."

"Really?" Rick said, pausing to take it all in. . . .

"Oh my God, that's great. I hope it's a girl!"

I couldn't believe how thrilled he was. I thought he might be freaked out, but he was excited. I was the freaked-out one!

Then I dropped the next bomb.

"Well, guess what? We're getting married."

I guess he thought I was joking because he burst out laughing. "Oh yeah, sure."

"Laugh all you want. We're getting married."

I don't think he ever said okay. I just took over. He knew me well enough by then to know I wasn't going to be some single mother. Besides, he had already told me: "If I don't marry you, I am not going to marry anybody else."

I got off the phone with Rick and made the most stressful call of the day—to my mom, who was in the same hotel, staying right down the hall.

# CHAPTER
## 23

I was relaxing in a nice hot bubble bath after a day on the set of *The Courage to Love*. I was thinking about all the fun I'd been having the last few days in Montreal. I had a small part in the ballroom scene, where I played an extra—a lady trying to find a wealthy gentleman for her daughter. Diahann Carroll, one of my all-time favorite actresses, stood next to me and we talked in between scenes and became fast friends. We'd gone out for drinks, chatted, and laughed. She was down-to-earth and just a lot of fun to be around.

But the best part was that I was able to "work" with my children. It was so nice to be around them and watch them in their element.

I was relaxed and happy in that warm bubble bath, so when the phone rang it startled me. I picked it up.

It was Vanessa. "I have to tell you something—I'm coming to your room."

Oh no! What could it be this time? All the tranquillity I had just experienced was wiped away by the urgency in Vanessa's voice. I knew this was something important.

But what?

Seconds later, Vanessa knocked on my door. We were staying down the hall from each other at a lovely boutique hotel.

She greeted me with a big smile. "Guess what?"

". . . Yes?"

"I'm pregnant."

"WHAT?"

"And Rick and I are going to get married."

I paused, trying to comprehend all this information. Pregnant and getting married? My first reaction was "But why?"

"Because I'm pregnant."

"So? Do you really have to get married? Do you really think that's the right decision?"

I'm really not a modern woman, but I just felt like, okay, you're going to have this baby, but you really don't have to marry him. I'm a traditional woman. I believe in marriage—I just didn't believe in this marriage. I didn't think Vanessa had given any thought to what it would be like to be the wife of a professional basketball player. I was not happy about this one bit.

To be honest, I knew it would never last, so I didn't feel the need to say anything more than I did.

Rick seemed too immature to me. Rick needed to be the Star. Rick didn't want to be known as someone's husband, which became a problem when people would eventually refer to him as "Rick Fox, who is married to Vanessa Williams." Well, that became one of the many problems.

I kept my mouth shut. I just figured, let it play out.

"Well, you're the one who's going to have to tell your dad."

But as soon as she left the room, I called Milton and told him. He was very calm about it. I think he felt as I did. Vanessa would do what she would do.

"That's her decision," Milton said.

But please! Ramon was thirteen years older. Rick was six years younger. Couldn't she just find someone in the middle?

When Diahann Carroll found out on the set the next day, she said

## MY MOST SHOCKING MOMENTS WITH VANESSA

- When Vanessa called to say she won Miss Syracuse. We had no idea what this meant and how it would eventually change our lives.
- When Vanessa won Miss America. We had told her that we didn't even think it was possible, but there she was—defying the odds and making history.
- When Ramon came into the house and told me he wanted to marry Vanessa. I thought, *But she's so young!*
- When Vanessa called to tell me she and Ramon were getting divorced.
- When Vanessa told me in one fell swoop that she was going to marry Rick Fox and that she was pregnant! What? And I had just come out of a nice, relaxing bubble bath.
- When I walked in on Vanessa and Bruce naked on the couch. Oh my God! I still haven't gotten over that one!
- Of course, finding out about the naked photos. But that could fill a book!

to me, "WHAT? She's going to marry him? Are you kidding me? He's beautiful, but he's a baby."

I said, "You tell her that. She doesn't listen to me."

By the way, if you're looking for my big acting debut in *The Courage to Love*, it wound up on the cutting-room floor! I guess knowing the producer doesn't always help.

*Can't you just have a baby and live together? Why do*
*you have to marry him?*

—HELEN WILLIAMS

My mother didn't understand that I wanted to do the right thing.

As wild as I may seem, I'm a traditional kind of girl. I want the whole package. I thought of the situation. I thought of my three children. Could I really be the pregnant single mom picking them up at school? I didn't think so. I couldn't imagine being a single mom with a baby. And why shouldn't we get married? Rick and I loved each other.

It didn't start out that way. I thought this would just be a fling with a gorgeous younger man, but I grew to love him more deeply than I thought I would. I fell in love with a man who was beautiful inside and out.

Even my mom had liked Rick—at first. When she met him, she was transformed into that giddy teenager I saw in her when I introduced her to Joe, my gorgeous bodybuilder boyfriend.

But mom's "love affair" with Rick quickly faded. And I blame myself. I committed a major faux pas—I told my mom about a fight Rick and I had early on in our relationship. Rick had accused me of flirting with another man, which led to a major blowout. At the time I thought, *Good riddance*. I was too angry to think clearly and I truly believed our relationship was done. I complained to my mom that Rick was too immature, too out of touch with his emotions, too jealous, too explosive. She listened but didn't say much.

But then Rick and I worked it out. Mom said, "Oh no, this isn't good." And shortly after, when I became pregnant, she was like, *OH NO!* She didn't say it, but it was written in bold letters across her face. Mom can never hide how she feels.

But come on—I wasn't the twenty-year-old looking for my parents' approval. I was thirty-six. Rick was financially established, so Mom knew if I wanted to take a break from work, he'd take care of me. He was not some random guy who impregnated me.

I always tell my mom too much—even she would agree with that. She says I share too much information with everyone—my friends, my children, even the press (a big change from what I was like after the "scandal"). But the problem is that Mom remembers *everything*. I'll get over it, forgive and forget. But Mom is a lioness, always protecting her cubs. Even if her cub is a woman with kids of her own!

I jumped right into wedding preparation mode. Rick and I had hardly any free time. I was in the last week of shooting *The Courage to Love*. Then I was off to Dallas for the first of my many commitments. After that, I had to jump in to star in *Shaft*, John Singleton's remake of the seventies blaxploitation classic.

Rick had to head to preseason training camp in three weeks. We had only a tiny window to pull this off.

Any time I wasn't on the set, I had Gena calling wedding planners and Vera Wang. On a day off, Gena and I picked out my engagement ring at Kaufmann de Suisse, a boutique in Montreal. It was a beautiful pale yellow princess-cut with two baguettes on the side. The store had someone fly to Los Angeles and drop the ring off with Rick.

As soon as the movie wrapped, I headed to New York to finalize the details.

Everyone flew in for our wedding rehearsal dinner. Rick met me in New York. I'm sure he hated the way I took control but I had no other choice. After our dinner, Rick had the driver drop me off at the Trump Plaza. I got out of the car and a homeless woman sprinkled green M&M's at my feet. *Odd*, I thought. I went to the front desk and a key was waiting for me.

I walked into the suite and was startled. Rick had decorated the entire place with memorabilia from our time together. He had saved every photo, restaurant menu, ticket stub, plane ticket, wine-bottle label, and matchbook. He must have spent the entire day turning that room into a museum of our relationship. If this were a scene in a movie, you'd think, *This guy is a crazy stalker—red flag! Red flag!* But it melted my heart.

I had no idea Rick had saved so much and was so sentimental. Halfway through looking at all the memorabilia, I cried. I couldn't believe I had such a sensitive man who had documented our entire relationship.

Then he got down on one knee, put the ring on my finger, and asked me to marry him. He said, "My love for you is so deep that you'll never know how much I love you."

It was a fairy-tale night.

*This was completely Rick's wedding. There were one
hundred guests, but I think I knew maybe twenty people.
It was all his family, his friends, his business associates.
I walked around, looking at these people and wondered
who they all were. Was I supposed to know them? It
didn't feel like it was Vanessa's day at all.*

—HELEN WILLIAMS

If you had attended our wedding, you'd have probably left smiling,
thinking you'd just been to a perfect affair. And it had seemed pretty
perfect. I wore a stunning Vera Wang gown with a taupe satin bod-
ice and a full tulle skirt (completely different from the straight
cathedral-length wedding gown I'd worn for my first marriage),
while Rick stood next to me, looking gorgeous in his Rick Pallack
tuxedo. We exchanged vows at the Church of the Holy Trinity, a
Byzantine-style church on the Upper West Side of Manhattan. Ivory
roses draped the altar, while thick cream-colored candles twinkled
from iron candelabras. The aisles overflowed with columns of
creamy roses and lush greenery.

Chris was my "maid of honor," Jillian and Melanie were bridesmaids, and Devin and Kyle were ring bearers. After we'd gone

through about half the ceremony, Deacon Tom Morrette announced, "Vanessa has a special gift for Rick."

I could barely contain my excitement. Rob Mathes, a friend and my brilliant musical director, walked up to the altar, sat down at the piano, and played the opening chords to a song he composed. Then he began to sing the lyrics—they were the words Rick had written to me in a poem "Today and Everyday," about how he knew when he first met me that I would one day be his wife. (Yes, Rick Fox wrote poetry for me!) Right after we had become engaged, I sent Rob the poem and asked him to set it to music and sing it at my wedding.

> *Today and everyday, I am yours for all time*
> *Today and everyday, like a miracle, baby, you are mine*
> *And though the winds may blow us far, far away*
> *Don't you forget my promise, listen to what I say*
> *I'm yours today and everyday.*

It slayed Rick. It was a very emotional moment for everyone. Rick cried, as did the entire audience. I was teary-eyed but I couldn't stop smiling. My gift had completely blown him away.

Later the reception was held on the St. Regis Hotel's top floor on a gorgeous Indian-summer day in September. Since Rick had been raised in the Bahamas, the reception had a Caribbean vibe. Guests danced to a steel-drum band and ate authentic Bahamian food— conch salad and guava duff fritters. For our song, Rick had chosen R & B singer Kenny Lattimore's "All My Tomorrows." We'd listened to it a lot over the last few months and it had become our song. So we walked into the ballroom and had our first dance as husband and wife—and Kenny was there to serenade us. Rick had completely surprised me. It was a fantastic moment and I had not expected it at all. The ballroom, showered in pink mood lighting, looked like a Caribbean paradise.

Then the toasts started—the best men, a few friends . . . and Mom.

Mom congratulated Rick on becoming part of our wonderful family. "We love our daughter very much. Welcome to the family." She didn't say a word about Rick. She had a big smile plastered on her face but her eyes were blazing so much they canceled out the smile. Then she said, "This has been a very short journey. Hopefully it will become a long journey."

The next day Rick headed to training camp. And I was in Chappaqua with my kids. We'd begun our lives together as a bicoastal couple. Could we make a relationship work if we'd barely see each other? And how much of a presence would Rick be in our baby's life? Was I about to be a single mom even though I was married?

Beware: When a man laughs when you say, "We're getting married," that's a good sign that there will be issues.

# CHAPTER 26

I was at Vanessa's house for lunch when she and Rick said that they were getting divorced. I knew already. I had heard through a friend that Rick had gone to the press to announce he had filed for divorce—before he even told Vanessa!

Rick's announcement had come totally out of the blue and caught me by surprise. I never thought the marriage would work, but the way Rick handled it shocked me. It was just a horrible thing for him to do. Vanessa had given the marriage her all. She'd been such a dutiful wife, traveling back and forth to Los Angeles and going to all his basketball games. I knew that Vanessa had wanted this marriage to work and she was probably devastated that he'd gone so public with the divorce. I was really, really upset for her.

He was sitting down in a chair off the kitchen and I just looked at him and couldn't take it anymore. I was so furious. My body felt like it was just shaking with rage. I walked up to Rick and gave him a good whack on the back of his head.

Of course I didn't hurt him. But I couldn't express my disappointment in words and there was his head—just available—waiting for me to whack it. I've never had an urge to whack someone's head like that before.

I whacked it. I didn't say anything. I walked away.

It felt good.

I think I got my point across.

*Vanessa loves being married. She just needs to find*
*someone who's mature and self-assured. Of course,*
*he has to be employed and/or financially secure. The*
*money factor is important at this stage of her life.*
*She needs someone who can take care of her for a*
*change—instead of her always being the caretaker.*

—HELEN WILLIAMS

I stared out at the turquoise ocean from my balcony on the twenty-eighth floor of the Continuum, where I was renting an apartment while shooting the television series *South Beach* in 2006, and I thought, *Okay. I hear it. Rick doesn't want to be married. I have to let go.*

It was one of those rare aha moments in my life, when suddenly everything becomes so crystal clear. I stood facing the South Beach action with the warm wind blowing through my hair. I closed my eyes and took a deep cleansing breath. For the first time in a very long time, I felt at peace.

Men tell you the truth—you just have to be willing to listen, I realized. And that truth was that Rick didn't want to be married to me anymore. I'd been in denial for a long time—too long. My marriage to Rick had been over for more than a year. He had served me with divorce papers at my home—what more proof did I need? But I convinced myself that we could work it out. We'd tried couples therapy, but we couldn't get it back.

Rick had told me he had a crush on me since he was a freshman at the University of North Carolina. He told me that there was no end to his love for me. He said I was the only woman he wanted to marry—ever. Now he was saying it was over. He wasn't the marrying kind of guy.

Instead of listening to him, I thought I could change his mind. I thought if I waited long enough, he would snap out of this phase and become the Rick who was madly in love with me.

Now, instead of praying that Rick would want me again, I prayed to thank God:

*Thank you God for all of my blessings and shine your light on me to help me carry out my path here on Earth. Make my children always feel my presence and direction and never let them feel abandoned.*

When Sasha Gabriella was born on May 1, 2000, Rick flew in from the road for the birth and held my hand during my scheduled Caesarian section (I had fibroid surgery a few years earlier and had to have a C-section). Rick played James Taylor music to relax us. The children were also at the hospital, excitedly awaiting Sasha's birth. I felt like we were one big happy family.

But the next day he flew back to Sacramento because the Lakers were in the playoffs. He played basketball wearing the hospital bracelet with FOX, GIRL, stamped on it.

Kathi picked me up at the hospital and drove Sasha and me home.

I had thought about moving to Los Angeles to be closer to Rick, but I didn't want to uproot the kids, who were settled in their schools; stability was my top priority for them. They'd been through enough already. Besides, Rick could get traded and then what? We'd have to move again.

Could the marriage have survived if we were in the same city all the time? Who knows. I thought I could make up for the distance by flying to Rick every other week (when the kids were with Ramon). During the off-season, Rick stayed in Chappaqua. But during the season, I was always flying back and forth. The traveling was exhausting, but I wanted us to be as normal a family as possible. I would arrange my calendar around his games and the children's activities.

Looking back, I have my share of regrets. When Rick was playing in the NBA championship against the Indiana Pacers at the Staples Center I didn't go to the games. Sasha was a newborn and I thought about taking her. Then I reconsidered. *Will it be too noisy? Too unsanitary?* I decided the traveling would be too difficult. But maybe I should have made the effort. Maybe I should have figured a way to

## HELEN ON BASKETBALL

I was never a fan of the sport. Actually, Milton and I really weren't avid fans of any sport. But I tried to be a supportive mother-in-law, so we'd go to the games when we were in Los Angeles. Milton would get bored, so he'd take one of his books to the Staples Center and sit there, reading. I didn't watch the game much, either. I'd look for the celebrities. One of my favorite moments was having my picture taken with Shaq. He's so tall—I think I came up to his elbow. I love that picture and I still have it on my corkboard in the kitchen.

make it work. His family was there for his first championship and I took photos of the win on the TV. It was Jillian's eleventh birthday and we were screaming when the Lakers won.

Right after the game, I talked to Rick on the phone. He was so happy and excited. I felt guilty for not being there to support him and celebrate with him. I also missed the parade in downtown Los Angeles to celebrate the Lakers' first championship since 1988. I was shooting a big Radio Shack commercial. I had a contract—I couldn't blow it off. I had to do the responsible thing. Devin and Kyle were there, but I regret missing out on such a major event in Rick's life. I was there for the next year in Philly and the year after that, when the Lakers played the New Jersey Nets.

But there were a slew of other events one of us always seemed to miss: Tony nominations, basketball games, birthdays, milestones in Sasha's life—first steps, first teeth, first words.

In our fifth year there was a shift in our relationship.

A tabloid had published questionable photos of Rick at training camp in Hawaii—with a blonde.

"It's better for you if you're not married to me," Rick said. "You don't deserve this at all, so I'll let you be single so you don't have to deal with me."

What? He was trying to end our marriage by pretending he was doing me a favor. But I believed marriage was forever. I wasn't giving up that easily. We had a daughter. We had our vows. I wasn't going through a divorce again.

As crazy as this may sound, I believed we could work through this. I believed Rick when he said nothing happened with the blonde in the photos. He went back to Los Angeles, back to the Lakers, and back to therapy. I went back to my illusion that if I tried harder, I could make everything all right. I could make him remember his love for me.

Professionally it had not been a great year for Rick. The Lakers did not "fourpeat." Rick had been beset by foot and neck injuries. He had had surgery and was on the bench for a big chunk of the season. Then he had spent the summer rehabilitating, but he never fully recovered. He developed bulging discs in his neck that affected his back. That summer he was traded to the Boston Celtics, the team where he had begun his career. He ended up retiring a few months later.

I got a call from Rick at 11:55 A.M. on August 19. He told me he'd gone to see his lawyer that day and filed for divorce. He said he wanted me to know because it would be announced the next day on ESPN. But just five minutes later it appeared on the ESPN scrawl.

RICK FOX FILES FOR DIVORCE FROM VANESSA WILLIAMS.

Rick's publicist, Staci Wolfe, made a statement to the *National Enquirer*: "They are heading for a divorce and have been so for the last eighteen months. They've virtually been leading separate lives."

Wow! That was news to me. The last eighteen months? Really? How come I didn't know anything about this? I knew things weren't great, but I had no idea they were horrible for so long. Here was some publicist talking about our marriage like she's an expert on it.

I called my lawyer to strategize. "It's not irreconcilable differences because I don't want to get divorced. So no, I'm not going to agree to that," I said. I wanted Rick to realize all that he was giving up—his wife, and especially his daughter.

In another twist of fate, the next album I was scheduled to record was filled with love songs. So that fall, I had gone to the studio to record tracks for *Everlasting Love*. The CD comprised mostly love songs from the 1970s—Jackson 5's "Never Can Say Goodbye," Stevie Wonder's "Send One Your Love," and Melissa Manchester's "Midnight Blue."

I was singing about love when the man I loved didn't love me anymore. Talk about pain!

I had also decided to put "Today and Everyday"—Rick's wedding poem—on the CD. Was I trying to torture myself?

What had once been a love song had become so bittersweet.

When it was time to sing it, I took a very deep breath and concentrated on the melody and my breathing. I tried not to picture us at the altar. The words that had been so beautiful, so full of hope, of love, of promise, now felt just plain sad.

> *Today and everyday, I am yours for all time*
> *Today and everyday, like a miracle, baby, you are mine*
> *And though the winds may blow us far, far away*
> *Don't you forget my promise, listen to what I say*
> *I'm yours today and everyday.*

I thought about all this as I sat on the balcony of the twenty-eighth floor of my apartment on a moonlit night in Miami. That song had been a gift from Rick to me. And even though Rick was gone, that song would always be mine.

*Rick with Sasha on the beach in the Bahamas, September 2000*

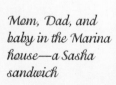

*Mom, Dad, and baby in the Marina house—a Sasha sandwich*

# PART FIVE

# SAVE THE BEST FOR LAST

# CHAPTER
## 28

*But he's such a good man. He's such a good, good man.*

—HELEN WILLIAMS

I thought my father would live forever.

Dad was one of the healthiest people I knew. He was active every day—chopping wood, mowing the lawn, and gardening. He'd have oatmeal for breakfast and snack on peanuts and raisins out of big jars he kept in the kitchen and in his car. Dad loved to bake wholegrain muffins with dried cranberries and bananas. He munched on the fruits and vegetables he planted in our garden in the backyard. My father was organic, eco-friendly, and green before it was trendy.

Dad had always been extra sensitive about his heart because his parents died so young—his mom, who struggled with high blood pressure, died of preeclampsia and a heart attack at twenty-eight, shortly after giving birth to her fifth child; and at fifty-three, his father also succumbed to a heart attack.

My dad wasn't going to be a victim of a bad heart, high choles-
terol, or high blood pressure. He did everything possible to stay
healthy for his family. And it worked—Dad rarely got sick. Dad was
strong and vibrant. Dad seemed invincible.

But it was more than just Dad's health that convinced me he'd be
around forever. My father was the leader of the Williams tribe—a
clan filled with artists, teachers, dreamers, and optimists. To me,
my dad was larger than life. I couldn't imagine a world without him
in it.

So when my mom called me in Miami on Saturday morning,
January 14, 2006, to say that Dad was really sick, I was shocked.
First, Dad didn't get really sick. And second, Mom wouldn't call if
Dad was going to be okay. She'd handle it herself and tell us about
it afterward. She thought she could take care of most situations and
wouldn't want to bother us.

But I didn't even recognize Mom's voice. She sounded panicked.

"You need to come," Mom said. "You need to come *now.*"

What? My heart started pounding. Mom sounded so unlike herself—could Dad's condition be *that* serious? How could this be happening? Thank God we were only a short forty-five-minute plane
ride away.

⁓

We went to the Bahamas for a party.

On Friday, January, 13, 2006 (yes, Friday the 13th), Milton and I
arrived in Nassau to celebrate a friend's sixtieth birthday. We'd had
a lovely Bahamian lunch with some dear friends at a restaurant.
Milton was full of energy, talking about his life, his children, his
grandchildren. That night, we continued the party with some
Chinese takeout at our friend's house. Halfway through the meal,
Milton got up from the table. In the kitchen he told me that his
stomach was bothering him.

Milton has always had a sensitive stomach and we'd mixed a lot of cuisines that day—conch for lunch, and egg rolls and a variety of Chinese foods for dinner. I put on the kettle and fixed Milton some mint tea. He sipped it, but it didn't stop the pain. Soon, he was doubled over.

We left the house and went back to our hotel, but he didn't feel any better. I called a doctor friend of our hosts who examined Milton in our hotel room and felt he needed to be admitted to the hospital. The doctors there said he had to stay overnight.

Then they administered tests.

"His pancreas is inflamed," they told me. This was more than just a bad stomachache, and I was concerned.

So I called Vanessa.

Fortunately, I was nearby—in Miami—for the National Foundation for Advancement in the Arts' YoungArts Week, where I was teaching master classes to seniors in high school who were scholarship finalists. (I'd also been a scholarship finalist in this program my senior year.) My television series *South Beach* was in limbo after being shut down because of hurricanes Katrina and Rita. I'd shot eight episodes and was waiting to hear if the show would continue or be canceled. I still had a few months left on my Miami apartment, so I invited Chris, my brother, to spend some time with me and the kids.

After Mom called, Chris, the kids, and I rushed to the airport and took the forty-five-minute flight to the Bahamas. I prayed the whole time we were on the flight that this would not be a big deal; that Dad would be on the mend and sitting up in his hospital bed by the time we got there. I thought about the last time I'd seen him—just two days ago. On Thursday, the mother of one of my parents' neighbors had died and we sat shivah with the family. My dad had baked sugar-free wholegrain muffins for them. We looked at old photos and reminisced. How could Dad have made muffins two days ago and be deathly ill now? It didn't make sense. He had to be okay. Dad was strong; he was a fighter; he would be fine.

There was the sound of my mother's voice echoing in my head. *"Your father's really, really sick."*

My mother never ever asks for help. It's not in her nature. She's tough. She's like steel. If there was a problem, she could handle it. Alone. But this time there was her silent plea to me. *I need you here. Help! I can't do this alone.*

It's always shocking when a parent needs their child, no matter how old the child is. Here I was, middle-aged, but I'd never heard Mom like this before. And it scared me.

When we arrived in Nassau, we rushed straight to the hospital. Dad was in a hospital bed.

He looked at me and said he was having a hard time breathing. I could hear the fluid in his lungs and it sounded like he was drowning. The doctors told us that his kidneys were failing and that his pancreas was inflamed. They told us that his situation was very serious.

Chris, Jillian, Sasha, Mom, and I surrounded Dad's bed. I stood next to him and squeezed his hand. What was going on? How could he suddenly be this sick?

"I can't breathe," he panted. "I feel like I can't breathe."

I stroked his hair and tried to calm him, but I didn't know what to say.

He couldn't catch his breath and his stomach looked swollen and distended. He was drowning in toxins. Mom had to make some serious decisions. We spoke to the doctors.

*What's the next step?*

"We can't take care of him here. Our facility just doesn't have what you need. He should be in a teaching hospital," a doctor told us. "We'll need to medevac him right away."

The doctors explained that my dad's pancreas was severely inflamed and his organs were shutting down. He had to be flown off this island as soon as possible. They said at this state of my dad's condition, acute pancreatitis, recovery takes a long, long time, and my dad could be in a hospital for months. "If he survives."

*If he survives.*

We got busy, calling on doctors we knew, trying to figure out which hospital would be the best place for someone with Dad's condition. In the end, the decision was up to my mother. She said she wanted him at Westchester Medical Center in Valhalla, which was only a few miles from home. So a neighbor of mine—Dr. Tony Pucillo, a cardiologist—made the arrangements to get him admitted there.

"If he's going to be in the hospital for months and months, it makes sense to have him near his house."

Then we had to do the most awful thing—place him in a medically induced coma. Dad was transferred by plane to the hospital.

We took a flight out of Miami to meet him there. We prayed that the doctors at this hospital would have the answers and everything would be okay. But we were terrified and in shock. We just couldn't understand how this was happening. Dad was supposed to be relaxing on a beach in the Bahamas. It was an out-of-body experience for everyone. We kept asking, "How? How?" How could Dad suddenly be so sick that doctors are telling us he might not survive? Dad might die? I couldn't even think about it.

When we met with the doctors in the intensive care unit, they looked grim.

"His heart's strong as ever, but all his organs are failing."

We stayed in his room. I squeezed his hand, rubbed his feet, and stroked his face. "Dad, we're all here," I said over and over. Mom was emotionally paralyzed, but in constant motion. She stared at him like she couldn't believe this was happening. She looked so lost and so frightened.

I could tell by the doctors' expressions that the situation was hopeless, but Mom wouldn't believe this. His organs were failing, but his heart was still strong, so that gave her hope.

"Oh, Milton, all that work on your heart. . . . The doctors told us your heart is still strong," Mom whispered to Dad, over and over.

The doctors performed an operation that basically sliced my dad's abdomen open. Later the doctors stopped by and told us what I already knew. "There's nothing else we can do."

How do you even comprehend those words? You don't. They make no sense. A few days ago, Dad was his normal self. Now he's in an intensive care unit and doctors are telling us the condition's hopeless. I felt sick and scared. It was just a matter of time, they said. He couldn't last very much longer.

After the doctors said there was nothing they could do, my mother burst into tears. "But he's such a good man. He's such a good, good man."

There was nothing worse than seeing my mother—so strong, so unflappable—look so helpless, so defeated, and so scared. I think sometimes she believed she was a handful for my father. There were times she felt like she didn't deserve such a remarkable man. He did everything right, so he should be allowed to live, not her, she thought. She loved him so much and couldn't fathom that the world she knew was suddenly ending. Chris and I wanted to protect her, but we didn't know what to do. We waited, we huddled, we brainstormed.

"Why him? Why him?" my mother kept repeating.

We stayed in Dad's room, praying he'd come out of it. Then on Monday night, Mom said, "Let's all go home and get some sleep."

The next morning, Tuesday, January 17, I woke feeling anxious. I had barely slept. I just tossed and turned while trying to grasp what was happening. My father was my idol, my hero, my model by

## HELEN ON MILTON

I thought Milton would bounce back because he always did. Why should this time be any different? He wasn't supposed to leave me. He said to me, "Don't worry, I'll always be here for you. I'll always be here." I couldn't even imagine that it was possible Milton would not survive. When the doctors told me his heart was strong, I really believed he would recover. I just couldn't imagine otherwise. Or maybe I just didn't want to imagine otherwise.

which I judged all other men. What would life be like without Dad in it? How could my mother continue without the man who had truly been her soul mate?

As night turned into morning, I lay in bed, thinking, *My dad is dead.* I felt like something in the world had shifted and would never be the same.

At 6:30 in the morning, the phone rang. I braced myself. Once I picked up that phone, everything would change.

It was my mother. "The hospital just called. It's your father . . ."

I didn't let her finish. I just couldn't hear the rest of the sentence. "I'm on my way."

I hung up the phone and got dressed as fast as possible. I said to Kathi, "Don't send the kids to school today."

I sped to the hospital in Valhalla. I ran past the front desk and took the elevator to Dad's room in the intensive care unit. As I raced down the ICU hallway, I saw a hearse out the window and prayed it wasn't an omen. I prayed that somehow Dad would still be alive.

But when I got to his room, the door was closed.

I took a long, deep breath and thought, *Okay. I can do this.* Then I flung open the door and walked in. The blinds were drawn. The equipment had been shut off, so there was no beeping of monitors or hissing of oxygen tanks. It was so quiet. So still.

And there was Papa.

Dad was lying on the bed. All the tubes and needles had been removed, but there was still a piece of tape on his mouth that had kept some tube in place. I walked over to him and stared at his lifeless body. "Oh, Dad," I said. I pulled off the tape, touched his face, and kissed him on the lips. I thought, *We have the same lips. They're the exact same shape.* Until that moment, I hadn't noticed.

"I love you, Dad."

Then the tears started pouring.

## BOOKS I RELIED ON THROUGH TOUGH TIMES

- *The Value in the Valley* by Iyanla Vanzant, an inspirational speaker and ordained minister. The book's message is that life is not just a series of peaks or mountaintop experiences but often a difficult journey through dark valleys.
- Thomas Moore's *Dark Nights of the Soul*, which deals with death, rebirth, and grieving. The theme of the book is that you should take the time to grieve—listen to sad music and cry. Don't be afraid of grief and don't suppress your sadness because then you will never get through it.

My mom slowly walked into the room. "Milton," she said in a voice that sounded completely devastated. I called Kathi and told her to bring the kids. They joined us as we huddled at Dad's bed, forming a circle around him.

*Why Dad? How did this happen? How could this happen? Why did this happen?*

We sobbed and sobbed. Our grief felt bottomless. Melanie cried so fiercely that her nose bled all over the floor.

I'd gone through two divorces. I'd known the pain of lost love, the agony of rejection. I thought I understood what it was like to be heartbroken. The moment I saw my dad's lifeless body, I realized I had no idea.

CHAPTER

29

The night before Milton died I whispered in his ear, "You can go now."

I didn't want to let go, but I had no choice. His organs had shut down, but I knew he was holding on for me, for his family. I knew I had to tell him that we'd be okay without him, even though I didn't necessarily believe that was true. I couldn't even imagine being without him. It sounds silly, but he promised he wouldn't leave me and I really believed him. For a while I was angry with him. How could he have done this to me? Of course it's irrational. One day I had this realization: "There's no choice. It's the natural progression of life." It was his time.

The night Milton died I went into my bed, just exhausted and so sad. I lay in our bed too tired to sleep. *Gosh, I'm alone now. There's no more Milton. He'll never be in this bed with me again to keep my cold feet warm.*

Suddenly I felt this incredible sensation of warmth. It was as if someone had taken a blanket and covered me with it, even though I was alone.

Milton.

I do believe that spirits are all around us. And I felt like Milton was sending me a message: Even though he wasn't in this world with us anymore, he'd still be there, looking out for us, keeping me warm.

In some way, he had kept his promise.

## MOMENTS I REALIZED MOM'S A ROCK STAR

- When Mom played piano at her beloved sister's funeral. Gretta was Mom's best friend; and two month earlier, my dad had died. So Mom was in deep, deep mourning. She played three different arrangements that were in her head and I was transported to another dimension while I watched in awe, amazed at her originality and talent. She didn't shed a tear. I have no idea how she did that. I know I couldn't have.
- At my father's memorial at the high school at which he taught, my mother stood up in front of the auditorium that was just packed with people. She delivered a eulogy that had everyone laughing and crying. She didn't have any notes—she spoke from her heart, even though she was filled with such sadness and even though she was still very much in shock.
- During the Miss America scandal my mother stood by my side and never lost her cool. She was a rock. I survived it because of Mom's support.

*Those were amazing acting skills on Vanessa's part
to develop that Wilhelmina persona. Where did those
glares, eyebrow raises, and "Don't mess with me"
attitude come from? I have no idea!*

—HELEN WILLIAMS

I had no desire to meet with producers of a pilot called *Ugly Betty*. I was so devastated by my dad's death that I needed some time. I was strong for my kids and tried to accept the loss, but I couldn't wrap my head around the fact that my dad was no longer with us. "Not a day goes by," as Sondheim wrote. There were countless times I'd head to the phone to call him, or flash on a thought that I wanted to share with him. Then I'd remember, *Dad's dead*, and a fresh wave of grief would slam into me.

Pilot season was in full swing. And the future of *South Beach*, the series I'd been working on, was uncertain. We'd shot the first eight episodes and were waiting for the back nine when I heard from a friend that the studio was selling off our set. That was a good sign that we weren't coming back.

My heart wasn't into it at all. But I also knew that keeping busy is what I do best—same thing with my mom. It's what keeps us from falling apart. It's the stillness, the silence that makes me remember what's going on in my heart.

A few weeks earlier I had met with writer/producer Candace Bushnell, the author of *Sex and the City*. She was gearing up to bring her new book, *Lipstick Jungle*, to television. I met with her because my manager said that the show would be shot in New York. If I was cast, I'd be able to stay in Chappaqua with my children. That sounded great, especially since I'd spent the last summer in Miami working on *South Beach*.

"My dad just died a few weeks ago. I wish I was just more up for this," I told Candace almost as soon as our meeting started.

"I understand. I just lost my mom," Candace said.

The meeting turned into a grief session. I think we were fighting back tears. After we talked about our parents' deaths, I did a quick, uninspired reading and was on my way.

I didn't get cast.

On the drive home, I remember thinking it might be time to give some serious thought to what was next. I needed to do something. It's a fact that you can easily get aged-out in this business. And here I was, just a few weeks from my forty-third birthday. While I've been blessed with the chance to express my talents in many different areas—from singing gigs to the Broadway stages—I was also aware that there were not many feature-film or television scripts on the horizon. The days of playing the young executive types were narrowing in my rearview mirror.

At this point in my career, I was reading for the roles of the moms, doctors, and lawyers. I could handle playing "Mom." I understood that there were certain roles you just one day grow out of. Besides, it didn't really matter what the parts were, as long as they were strong, character-driven roles.

Even before the *Lipstick Jungle* meeting, my manager had been pushing *Ugly Betty*, a television pilot that revolved around a fashion magazine, which was also slated to be a New York–based production. He got me a copy of the script and kept asking me to read it and take a meeting. He was persistent, almost relentless. He said the show's producers, including actress Salma Hayek, really wanted to meet me or at least get on the phone with me.

I'd just booked a trip to Egypt. I had been asked to sing at a friend's wedding and I decided to take Mom and the kids along during their winter break. A change of scenery was just what we all needed. We'd escape into the world of tombs, pyramids, camel rides, and adventure.

"But would you please get on the phone with them?" my manager asked.

"Hey, if my BlackBerry works while I'm sailing down the Nile, I'll certainly try to make that call."

I hadn't even gotten the part, but I was already channeling Wilhelmina!

Fierce!

This was my second trip to Egypt in a year. In August, a few months before my father died, my mom and I had toured the country with a few girlfriends. During the entire trip—whether we were exploring pyramids, touring museums, or cruising the Nile—we'd look at one another and say, "Dad would have loved this." He was such a history buff and the trip would have fascinated him. We felt guilty for not including him on the girls' trip. We realized we should have had him tag along and see the sights with us. So we returned as a family to a place my dad, the kids' Papa, would have loved. I had such a wonderful time that I didn't want to leave.

Oh, and as for the call to the *Ugly Betty* producers? I tried, but I couldn't get a decent signal. I shrugged off all those dropped calls as a sign from the universe. The producers and the network cast Wilhelmina. I enjoyed my trip and that was that.

Well, actually it wasn't.

The actress who was cast as Wilhelmina was let go. It's not un-common for producers to swap out actors and crew during and after a pilot. Legend had it that she showed up at a table read in huge sunglasses. She delivered her dialogue so quietly that it was impos-sible to hear a word she spoke. At the end of the table read, the network and the executive producers, Silvio Horta and Salma Hayek, decided to call me and make me an offer.

I got a call at ten thirty that night. My manager told me the job was mine—if I wanted it. He said they knew I would be perfect. After all, I have a history of nailing strong witchy characters—from Ebony Scrooge in *A Diva's Christmas Carol*, which VH1 runs every holiday, to my roles on Broadway in *Kiss of the Spider Woman* and *Into the Woods*.

I admit that when I finally got around to reading the script, I could not put it down. Wilhelmina leaped off the page, which is always a sign of brilliant writing. There was no question about how she would speak, the tone of her voice, or the way she would carry herself. What I loved most about the character is that she is color-less, strong, fierce, and formidable. She's running the show at a mainstream fashion magazine where she struts around in power pumps and killer suits. She lives in a world where fashion is every-thing—it's all about the hottest designer and the hottest colors and trends. There's no question that she deserves to be where she is. And race had nothing to do with her. It was an equal-opportunity show with plenty of accents, color, and attitude.

And Wilhelmina's eye-cutting stares? Her exasperation? Her don't-mess-with-me attitude? I didn't have to look far for inspiration. I'd just channel the person I knew longest and best.

Mom.

I didn't have time to ponder whether or not I was ready to do this. I'd have to start immediately—beginning with a wardrobe fitting the next day.

I've learned you never know when it's going to come. That's

become my prayer. *God, I surrender. Just show me the way and I will follow you. Let me see the signs.*

And those signs were relentless.

The next day, I showed up to do a fitting in the wardrobe trailer with the legendary fashion icon Patricia Field (the costume designer for *Sex and the City*). Wilhelmina's wardrobe had already been selected—for the previous actress, who was a size 2! I luckily squeezed into ivory separates. Patricia loved the way I wore the clothes. The official thumbs-up from the queen of fashion was good enough for me.

One of the gags on the show was that Wilhelmina Slater was so formidable that she couldn't keep an assistant. So there would be a new assistant each week who would be fired. For the pilot, a Juilliard-trained actor named Michael Urie was cast as Marc St. James, my assistant. The minute we started our scene together, I was blown away by this extremely talented young actor. You could throw anything at him and he would make it work. He was aware, intelligent, and willing to go for it.

I knew immediately that the two of us had some special chemistry. He was like my mirror. He'd capture my mood, my attitude and imitate it, so we became this one person, this one force. In our first boardroom scene, I slid into my chair in a particular way and Michael did the exact same move.

"Michael needs to be a series regular," I immediately told Silvio. The Botox scene in the pilot immediately cemented our friendship. Willie gives Marc the leftovers from her vial and Michael tapes up an eyebrow to make his brows lopsided. It was hilarious.

On the first day of shooting in my office, Salma Hayek sat next to the monitors with our young star, America Ferrera, the lead of the show, or #1 on the call sheet. Salma had fallen in love with America in *The Sisterhood of the Traveling Pants* and *Real Women Have Curves* and had fought for her to become Betty.

In between setups, Salma and America started giggling.

"We want to do something for you," they said, with these enormous grins plastered on their faces. I knew they were up to something.

"What?"

They burst out in song: "SOMETIMES THE SNOW COMES DOWN IN JUNE."

They sang "Save the Best for Last" in these really goofy voices. I loved it!

That was their way of welcoming me in.

"Very nice," I said, just like Arnold would say with a smile and a stogie.

From the beginning I knew that *Ugly Betty* was not going to be average. It looked different. Our director, Richard Shepard, shot it unconventionally. The show wasn't a drama and wasn't quite a comedy. As much as I loved the script and the set, I wondered, *Would viewers get it?*

After I wrapped my part, Salma called my cell. "Thanks so much. We really appreciate your being a part of *Ugly Betty*. You were great. You were so funny. You saved us."

I had gone from being indifferent about this project to really wanting it. A steady gig in New York? It was too good to be true.

I've learned over the years never to get too attached to anything in show business. So I went about my life—busy with the kids and traveling to Holland to guest star in *Musicals in Ahoy*, a huge Broadway-themed series of concerts that filled a Rotterdam arena for a nice run.

While I was there I got the news . . . the pilot got picked up! Yay!

And the show was moving to L.A.

WHAT? The whole idea was for me to live and work in New York.

I had four kids in four different schools. In the fall, Melanie was headed to the Fashion Institute of Technology (FIT), Jillian would be a senior at Greeley, Devin was in his last year of middle school, and Sasha was starting first grade at Montessori.

"I can't do the show. You told me it was a New York show and that's why I agreed to do it."

I'd already paid my dues flying between New York and Los Angeles while juggling motherhood and work. And I lost two marriages as a result.

I loved the part and I knew that I needed to get back to work, but that constant commute across the country was a grind. Was a bicoastal life worth it for a regular paycheck? I didn't think it was fair to put my family through that kind of strain again. Plus, it was L.A.—the site of two troubled marriages. I have a lot of mixed emotions about L.A.—fond memories of those early years with Ramon when my career was just taking off, and championship Laker moments with Rick. But it's also a place where I experienced a great deal of pain.

While shooting the pilot, I was the biggest "name" attached to the show. Most of the cast were also New York hires, so they turned to me to have me try and fight to keep it in town. But it was my decision—I couldn't leave my kids. The studio said, "We'll give you three days to reconsider. Then we'll have to cast again."

"Go ahead." And I let it all go.

I knew the producers weren't happy, nor was my manager, but I didn't back down.

I showed the pilot to the kids and asked them if I should do the show. Melanie spoke up for everyone. "Mom, it's a great role. We'll be fine. Do it."

The studio called me back. They'd give me a three-day workweek so I could fly home on weekends, plus I'd receive a relocation bonus for housing to accommodate my four kids and a nanny. And then I remembered what Melanie had said.

"We'll be fine. It's a great role."

Melanie had been an infant when I launched my career, so she's grown up watching me juggle work and motherhood. I can barely remember my life before I had children, so kids always came before a career. Sometimes I've done well, other times I felt like I'd failed. But here was my daughter—who as an infant toured the country with me, who went on auditions with me—giving me career advice.

I asked Ramon what he thought. "Do the show," he said. "We'll all handle it, don't worry."

I signed on the dotted line in May 2006. In July, I moved into a rental house in the hills of Bel Air. All the kids were in Chappaqua, under the watchful eye of their dad, Kathi, and Mom, except Mel who moved to the Chelsea section of Manhattan to be close to FIT. The next season I got a bigger house and moved Sasha to L.A. I hoped that now Rick and I were living in the same city, Sasha would get a chance to experience life with both of her parents. Everything was falling into place.

I was beginning the next chapter of my life.

# CHAPTER

## 31

*Milton would have loved watching Vanessa as Wilhelmina, but I don't think he would have appreciated some of the sarcastic humor in the dialogue. It would have been fun to explain it to him and watch him laugh with some hesitation.*

—HELEN WILLIAMS

I was you for Halloween."

I couldn't believe how many times I heard those words in the days following Halloween the first year *Ugly Betty* was on television. I'd get attention in restaurants and parking lots. People would yell on the street to tell me how much they loved Willie. It was "Bettymania." America Ferrera exploded as everyone's favorite underdog; Michael Urie was television's new funny man.

We'd struck a chord and developed a cultlike following. My mother and her friends loved the show for the style of it: *What will Willie be wearing this week?* Then there were the hardcore fashionistas who loved the haute couture and the glimpse into the world of a high fashion magazine. After all, real-life fashion insiders like Vera Wang, Kenneth Cole, Badgley Mischka, Nina Garcia, and Tim

Gunn all paid visits to the offices of *Mode* and gave the show an authentic vibe.

Lastly there were the underdogs—the tweens, teens, and young adults who could relate to Ugly Betty's plight, who knew Ugly Betty personally, because Ugly Betty was them.

People really responded to my character in a way I'd never experienced before. I'd started getting comments when I'd go through security at the airports. There were the gay men who loved my style and attitude. There were women my age and older who would come up to me and say, "Girl, I love you for being so bad," or "I hate you, but I love you." "Why you gotta be so mean?" To the latter, I would respond, "That's what I get paid to do" (with a smile). Then there were younger fans who'd treat me as if I actually was Wilhelmina! Sometimes it felt like there was a force field around me. I'd hear whispers and they'd look at me, too afraid to approach. I loved it because the truth is . . . I am nothing at all like Wilhelmina!

Sometimes I wished I lived like she did—her penthouse apartment was insanely posh! Having someone at my beck and call at any moment would be a luxury. I wish I could ask for something and it would just magically appear. But alas, it would begin to drive me crazy. I love my privacy too much. I love my independence. I love doing things for myself and for others.

*Ugly Betty* was a treat for four crazy years. I wore beautiful costumes by Thierry Mugler, Alexander McQueen, Halston, and Fendi. We shot at locations—the Bahamas, London, Times Square, the Guggenheim, on yachts, and in cemeteries. I acted on incredible sets with fabulous decor. (I got to take two chairs from Willie's apartment, two horse heads, and two lamps. Michael Urie has the signature glass desk from my office.)

Our cast was also so different from most television shows. Most of us had theater backgrounds, so we knew what it was like to work as an ensemble. We all were thankful for the work and the opportunity to stretch ourselves. We worked long hours. We survived the writers' strike, moving from New York to Los Angeles and back again. I know it sounds corny but we quickly became one big happy family.

Each week we'd have a screening of that Friday's episode of *Ugly Betty* on set. We'd watch the show together in our costumes and slippers during lunch and just laugh and cry. It was a treat to see the whole show put together with music.

I was busy working fourteen-hour days. I was shooting the show and doing interviews and posing for photos to promote the show. On my days off, I'd drive Sasha to school and activities. At night I'd practice my lines—highlighting and making notes with Sasha in bed next to me. She'd play Marc and I'd be Wilhelmina. Whenever she laughed, I'd think, *Oh, this is going to work.* This became our own version of a bedtime story. When Sasha watched the show, she'd get excited when she recognized the lines she had rehearsed with me.

I was enjoying Los Angeles. The show was a hit, Sasha had received her First Communion, the family was visiting, and Rick was back in Sasha's life. He even made a cameo on *Ugly Betty* (he played Willie's bodyguard and they hooked up).

It was a sunny Sunday afternoon when the phone rang. I was outside on the patio. Sasha was jumping on the trampoline and Mom was reading the Sunday *New York Times*. It was Silvio Horta, the producer. Calling me on a Sunday? *Uh oh. Am I getting fired?*

"I've got some great news—the show's moving back to New York," he said. "I know you'll be the happiest of everyone."

He explained the benefits of the city's 35 percent tax break for local productions. The show would save up to fifteen million dollars per season, he said.

*You've got to be kidding me. I'd just gotten used to Los Angeles.*

I felt like the wind had been knocked right out of me. Was I really being asked to uproot my life for a second time in as many years? Crazy how life works.

I finished my last week of shooting at Raleigh Studios and packed up for Tennessee, where I was playing Miley Cyrus's agent in *Hannah Montana: The Movie*. (How could I refuse—Sasha was a huge fan and I was "the coolest mom" in her eyes.)

I had to continue recording my next CD, *The Real Thing*. I called New York and enrolled Sasha in a school. As for the home I had rented? Lara Spencer just had gotten a deal as the host of the television show *The Insider*. She had to move to Los Angeles and needed a place. Perfect. She moved into my rental house, which was already furnished with the furniture Rick had given me from our Marina house. Thank God for Brian Edwards, my client relations executive. He handled all the details so smoothly—like he always does.

Then it was back to Queens for *Ugly Betty*.

*From Atlantic City to L.A. to New York and everywhere in between—thirty years later and Brian Edwards is still my right-hand man. Who the hell would have thought?*

*Receiving my star on the Hollywood Walk of Fame with Brian*

# CHAPTER
## 32

Vanessa loves performing, but she's happiest when she's with her children. She's very generous with them—almost to a fault. They seem to get everything they want and ask for.

Vanessa is a very kind and giving person. She works very hard and as a single mom she's always had some guilt for not always being there. But she makes a point of being there for all the important events. She'll fly across the country for a birthday or a play or one of the kids' sporting events. Once, she flew home from Japan so she wouldn't miss Jillian's confirmation, and flew back the next day to continue her concert schedule.

Sometimes I worry that they don't appreciate everything Vanessa's been able to provide for them to make growing up comfortable and easy. They expect it because that's just how they were raised. My concern is that they're used to such a privileged quality of living that it may be a challenge for them to provide for themselves when

## PARENTING TECHNIQUES:
## HELEN VERSUS VANESSA

**VANESSA:** I made a decision when I was pregnant with Melanie that I'd always be honest and open with my kids. I don't have inhibitions about sharing information with them, whether it's about me or if there's something they've seen on television that they have questions about. I've told them about the mistakes I've made in my life, my marriages, as a parent, and what I've learned from them. I want them to know who I am as a person, a woman, and as their mother. That's not something that I got at home growing up. I don't want to be weighed down by secrets. I want my children to know me, to like me, and to eventually be my friend.

**HELEN:** To me being a good parent is a lot of trial and error. In hindsight, what worked for us as parents was being consistent in family rules, establishing clear expectations, and setting positive goals. The priority for us was being a parent and showing our kids that they are loved. Friendship was secondary. I didn't care if I was my child's friend. But as my children have aged into adulthood, I'd like to think they think of me as their mother *and* their friend. Although Vanessa doesn't have to share everything with me! (Unless, of course, it's good gossip!)

they have to survive on their own. I have no doubt that they're talented and smart enough to do it, but it won't be easy. Just ask Vanessa. I've decided that in my next life I want Vanessa to be *my* mother.

# CHAPTER

## 33

*Vanessa's children are all very creative. But if they decide to go the singing or acting route, I think it is important they remember who their mother is and know it may be hard to live in that celebrity shadow.*

—HELEN WILLIAMS

With the grace of a seasoned athlete, Sasha leaped into the air, arched her back, swung her arm, and spiked the volleyball over the net, scoring a point for her team. And the crowd of parents assembled in the Curtis Elementary School gym burst into rowdy applause.

"Yay, Sasha! Good job!" someone yelled when the applause died down.

With a big grin on her face, Sasha turned and sought out the voice. "Thank you," she said.

A few of the mothers sitting near me grinned. "Who does that? one asked me. "What kid says thank you while they're in the middle of a game?"

Sasha does. When I watch her play her favorite sports—whether volleyball, basketball, softball, or swimming—I am so proud. Not because of her skill—although she's athletic like her father—but because that girl is just so joyous. She's this amazing confection of silliness and intensity; and I marvel as the other kids seem to gravitate toward her energy.

Someone this happy, this full of joy and light, hasn't suffered because of the choices I've made; in fact, she's thrived.

I've questioned whether my career decisions would affect my children. Do I move? Do I stay? Can the kids handle the instability? How much school will they miss?

Sasha has been affected the most by the vagaries of my career. She moved to Los Angeles with me for *Ugly Betty* and she moved back to New York with *Ugly Betty*. Then when *Ugly Betty* was canceled, she returned to Los Angeles for *Desperate Housewives*. And after *Desperate Housewives* ends this season? Who knows? Maybe we'll stay, maybe we'll return to New York. I could worry about the effect this constant state of flux could have on such a young life.

But Sasha is resilient.

"So what, Mom? If I go to another school, it's okay." Sasha blurted this out one day when asked about the unsure future. Then she shrugged and gave me a reassuring smile. "I make friends easily. It will not be a big deal. You don't have to worry about me."

What more could a mother want from life than to have children who tell her that she doesn't have to worry about them? Of course as a mom, I will always worry—that's what we do. Ask my mother—she still worries about Chris and me. But the truth is, I have four amazing children who are becoming amazing adults. They are strong-minded, high-spirited, and brimming with talent.

They are, without question, my greatest accomplishment.

I started having children so young that I've never really known what it's like not to have them around. I'll listen to some parents talk about their kids and some speak like they're such a burden. They'll ship them away to summer camp any chance they get. I love having my children together in my house, eating a big homemade lasagna dinner and bonding over childhood memories. I love hearing their laughter. Typical of their ages, the kids love to poke fun at the grown-ups. It's not unusual to have both Ramon and Rick over to dinner. They once took the kids skiing while I was in Miami. How's that for teamwork? It's truly a blended family, complete with Rick's son, Kyle.

Right now Sasha's the only one at home. I have no idea how I'll adjust when they're all out of the house. By that time, I may have grandkids running around. It's not that crazy—I made my mom a grandmother when she was exactly my age now.

Melanie, the uptown girl, has the heart of a writer. Even as a child, her poetry was deep and mature. She has a wonderful voice. She sang a solo, "Gracious Good Shepherd," on my first Christmas CD. She's danced her whole life and is a great mimic. Yet, she is such a private person and never likes to be the center of attention. She's in Manhattan, living the dream—she writes a fashion blog, has a real estate license, and works as a fashion stylist. I always ask her for recommendations on clothes. She chose my gowns for the Emmys and helps dress me for photo shoots. She has a great eye and a terrific sense of fashion. Even as a toddler, she would kick off denim; insist on silky nightgowns; and beg for pretty dresses, party shoes, and tights.

Jillian, my downtown girl, is living *my* dream. She's dancing in a modern company, rehearsing at Alvin Ailey, and enjoying all that the city has to offer. Like Melanie, Jillian's been a dancer her whole life and majored in dance at the New School, where she graduated last year. Her style of dance would be considered alternative and I'm thrilled that she can be a pro at it. She also sings and writes music. She sang with me during my concert tour in Japan this past summer. I hosted the Daytime Emmys in 2009 and got choked up when I sang my opening number, "The Sweetest Days," a song written about my kids. I look over and there's Jillian onstage with me singing backup.

Devin just started freshman year in college. He's a man of few words but I follow him on Twitter to keep up. How modern! He also is athletic, a great dancer, and a sax player. He writes and produces rap music. Devin is an impeccable dresser. Even as a young boy his shirt, pants, and sneakers all had to match. "I'm the red Power Ranger today!" The next day, he'd be the white Power Ranger. Then the blue Power Ranger. He had Power Ranger birthdays four years in a row. His Power Ranger obsession eventually ended, but his obsession for coordinating his style never did.

He's also a natural onstage. His last performance was when he played Birdie in his middle school's production of *Bye Bye Birdie*. He'd watched me play Rosie in the 1995 ABC television version. So he auditioned for Birdie to surprise me and got the lead. I saw his performance twice when I flew in from the *Betty* set. He was a sensation. But that was his last musical. "It's not my thing," he told me. He played saxophone (my father taught him) at his high school graduation. But as he performed, I thought, *That's the last time I'll ever hear him play. He's done with that, too.* My dad would have been so proud. I'm sure somewhere Papa was smiling.

Through it all, Ramon and Rick and I have managed to strike up solid friendships and respect for one another. We're all there for birthdays, graduations, Thanksgivings, Christmases, Easters. We've all stayed at my house together with both men in the guestrooms and the kids beaming. Last year, Ramon was in between houses and he needed a place to live, so he stayed with us in Chappaqua for months. Why not? It was weird and awkward at times, but the kids loved it. Ramon's a great cook and an obsessive cleaner, which are great benefits. Plus, he's been almost a stepdad to Sasha, attending dance recitals, basketball games, and swim meets, and joining us at mass.

Silvio came to visit me in my trailer on location to give me the news of *Betty*'s cancellation in its fourth season. It was so sad. America and I were shooting a really funny double-dating scene and we had to pretend that our hearts weren't breaking. But even though I

## HELEN ON BEING VANESSA'S NEIGHBOR

I'm getting older. It's comforting for Chris and Vanessa to know I'm living next to one of them. Now they don't have to worry so much about me. Not that there's anything to worry about—I'm in great shape, I exercise every day and I feel wonderful. But I am in the fall of my life on this earth and it was time for a change. Even though Milton told me he'd never leave our Millwood home, I know he would have wanted me to move. He would be happy knowing I'm so close to Vanessa. I'm pleased that I've done it—it was a huge accomplishment for me to move out of the house that had been my home for forty-eight years, then design and build my new house.

And Vanessa and I don't see each other all the time—only when we want to, which is the perfect arrangement.

As I age it's nice to reflect on my children, grands, and where my journey has led me thus far. I hope what lies ahead will be positive experiences but what I know for sure is . . . you have no idea!

was upset, I was lucky—I still had work. James Lapine (who had directed me in *Into the Woods*) asked if I wanted to do a limited run at the Roundabout Theatre in a show about Stephen Sondheim's life.

James Lapine had created an incredible evening that allowed the audience to travel through Stephen Sondheim's brilliant career as a lyricist, composer, son, student, and Broadway icon. I would get stage time with Barbara Cook, the legendary soprano now in her eighties, who sounded like she was still in her prime—just smokier.

I loved to sit next to her and listen to her theater stories and then hear her curse at Stephen because the intervals were so tricky.

Barbara and I had a showstopping number together at the top of act 2. I was seated on a block on stage right, singing "I Think About You." Then on stage left, Barbara sings "Not a Day Goes By." We both stand up and walk toward each other, our songs overlapping. It builds into a crescendo and the house would go wild.

"Whoo-hoo, they love us," Barbara would squeal as we strolled offstage.

I met with Marc Cherry, creator of *Desperate Housewives*, at his suite at the Essex House Hotel in Manhattan. Every year after the show wraps, he visits New York for two weeks to catch up on all the new Broadway shows. Marc was a musical-theater major, too, so when we met, we immediately bonded over our shared loves— Sondheim, theater stories, and Miss America. He knew all about the pageant—the competition and the songs.

We talked a good forty-five minutes and then Marc asked if I'd seen *Desperate Housewives*. "I want you to join the cast."

We brainstormed. We threw some ideas around. Marc decided that my character would be a former New Yorker who was divorced but was once married to a New York Yankee. She'd constantly shock Wisteria Lane residents with her insensitive comments and behavior. She'd be funny and a force, but different from Wilhelmina. It sounded perfect to me.

Then Marc and I went back to talking about theater.

So Renee Perry was born one May day in the downstairs restaurant at the Essex House in between theater chat.

When I left, I did what I always do after these meetings—I called Mom.

"That sounds like a great idea, Ness," Mom said after I told her the latest. And I thought, *Okay, good, Mom wants me to do the show.* I still want Mom's approval.

My first meeting with the cast was a read-through at Marc's house. Everyone breezed in and embraced one another and told their summer vacation stories. They were about to begin their seventh year together and they were welcoming to me. And I was happy to have a job. Maybe I could boost their ratings by bringing in some of the *Ugly Betty* viewers who were in withdrawal. (Although, Wilhelmina would cringe if she saw some of Renee's get-ups!) I'd also bring back the black audience who hadn't seen a black main character since 2005 when Alfre Woodard was on the Lane and kept her son shackled like a slave in the basement.

It's great when people come up to me and say, "Renee cracks me up. . . . You are so funny." But even better is being on the set and making the crew laugh while they're watching. They'll hold it in until the director says, "Cut!" Then there's this roar of laughter. That's the moment I live for.

I've had a lot of those moments.

A few years ago, I starred as the Witch in a revival of Stephen Sondheim's *Into the Woods*. One day I'm rehearsing at the theater when I got the word that Stephen Sondheim decided he would rework "Last Midnight," which is the Witch's final, pivotal number. In this new version, the Witch would not only threaten the Baker and his wife but she would also take their baby and sing to it. This required more music and additional lyrics written by Sondheim for me!

There I am, at the theater waiting for Stephen to fax fresh lyrics. I flashed back to freshman year at Syracuse, when my friend Tim Thayer played Stephen's song "There Won't Be Trumpets" on the piano. I remembered the thrill of hearing this new music and learning about this brilliant composer. And now Stephen Sondheim's writing music and lyrics for my character!

At that moment I thought, *How crazy—from student and dreamer to now being able to live my dream. It has manifested.*

There aren't too many times in my life that I go, "Wow, I can't believe this is actually happening." Usually, I don't realize the enormity of a moment until it has already passed. But it always hits me eventually. The first time I sang my version of "Last Midnight," chills raced through my body. Just like they had the first time I sang with Barbara Cook or the first time I took over for Chita.

I thought to myself, *I'm part of Broadway history.*

I remember a conversation I had with Phil Stewart, my acting teacher from Horace Greeley. At the time, I was just about to star in *Kiss of the Spider Woman*. I was excited and proud, but I also was frustrated with some of the press who kept bringing up Miss America. We were talking about my career and I complained a bit to him.

"I'm finally on Broadway and getting rave reviews, but Miss America will never go away. It's always mentioned in articles, headlines, and descriptions of me."

He looked at me and smiled. "Well, I guess that was your path. You know it doesn't diminish your work. It doesn't take away from everything you've done. You just have to accept it as part of your journey, part of your history."

I realized he was right. Let it go. For better or worse, Miss America will always be a part of me. It doesn't define me, but it will always be a part of my story.

I flashed back to that moment when I was pregnant with Melanie and a reporter had asked what I'd tell my child about the Miss America scandal. At the time I was offended and speechless. His question echoed in my head for years and years. How could he ask me such a thing? What *would* I tell my children?

Now I know the answer to that question. Because when they asked about Miss America, those photos, or any other part of my life, I told them what I always tell them—the truth.

After all, it was part of my journey that led me to them and to where I am today.

I sang "Happy Birthday" to Stephen Sondheim for his eightieth, just before James Lapine surprised him with his own theater, New York, March 22, 2010.

Performing with the legendary Barbara Cook on Broadway in SONDHEIM ON SONDHEIM, *New York, 2010*

Performing my solo "Ah, But Underneath," from the second act of SONDHEIM ON SONDHEIM, *New York, 2010*

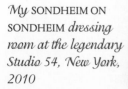

My SONDHEIM ON SONDHEIM *dressing room at the legendary Studio 54, New York,* 2010

*My* UGLY BETTY *dressing room at Silvercup Studios, New York, 2009*

*Lunch with the girls from* UGLY BETTY, *(left to right) Me, Judith Light, America Ferrera, Becki Newton, and Ana Ortiz, New York, 2010*

*Cohosting the ABC Inaugural Special in honor of President Barack Obama, Washington, D.C., January 2009*

*"Singet dem Herrn ein neues Lied (Sing Ye to the Lord)," Bach Motet 1 My mother with her college mentor, Dr. Richard F. Sheil*

# ACKNOWLEDGMENTS

Mom, you've provided me with the armor that gives me strength in my battles, the grace to make everything look effortless, and the humor to always look at life as a crazy unending adventure.

Dad, well, you get your own chapter in this book . . . not a day goes by that I don't miss and love you.

To my insanely talented brother, Chris, who is a wonderful example of a Williams man. Incredible shoes for you to fill and your best is yet to come.

To Ramon, for not only believing in me when many didn't but also giving me three gifts of life: Melanie, Jillian, and Devin.

To Rick, for cocreating our powerhouse daughter, Sasha Fox.

And of course thanks to my four most important and glorious productions, my children:

Melanie, you continue to unfold like a beautiful flower as you mature. I am so proud of your writing, your elegance, and your deep concern for others.

Jillian, you exude such passion for life! May it never cease and may you continue to not be afraid to take chances. And we can't forget your unique trait of bursting into tears at the sight of Chris Tucker or the thought of an injured Saint Bernard.

Devin, the most stylish son a mother could ask for. Your panache, love for the finer things in life, and music will take you far. I have no doubt all of your dreams will come true.

Sasha, your exuberance is infectious. You always give me a funny story to tell, your smile lights up a room, and I will always be your biggest fan in your fan club . . . superstar!

Irene, we did it between kids' schedules, the 101/405 chaos, and coast-to-coast sit-downs. Brava!

And the incomparable Brian Edwards, who is solely responsible for getting this book handed in on time! Your tireless effort, attention to detail, and quirky Southern phrases always charm the hell out of everyone you deal with. Your recollections are outstanding, and I couldn't have completed this without you at the helm. Thanks for your dedication, loyalty, and friendship through almost thirty years!

*Vanessa Williams*

To all the teachers who paved my life path for the love of music, books, and a desire to be a constant learner.

Brian Edwards, I could not do this without your guidance and detailed management skills.

Irene, you made the words flow in my voice.

My "peeps" (you know who you are) for the support and encouragement to make this project possible.

Big hugs, much love, and sincere "thanks" to you all.

*Helen Williams*

# SPECIAL THANKS

Debbie Allen; Chuck Amos; Gena Avery; Andrea Barzvi and Jennifer Joel at ICM; Betsy Berg; Kate Best; Amber Brockman, Alexandra Marcus, and the PMK-BNC Team; Brad Cafarelli, Lucian Capellaro; Diahann Carroll; Michael Chanslor and Viral Video; Kristin Chenoweth; Marc Cherry; Linda Chester; Bettina Cirone; Sam Fine; Lauren Feinstein and the Crush Brands Team; Geordie Frey; Liz Germano; Karen Gottlieb; Michael Gruber; Bruce Hanson; Sam Haskell; Jason Hoffman and the ABC/Disney TV Photo Department; Scott Hoover; Gary Jaffe; Oscar James; Mike Jelline and the UTA Team; Caytha Jentis; Travers Johnson, Beth Parker, Erica Ferguson, and the Gotham/Penguin Team; Scott Jones; Kyle Kogan; Andrew Leff and Kyle Whitney; Bonnie MacIsaac, Sharon Pearce, and Liz Puro; Ana Martinez-Holler, Johnny Grant, and the Hollywood Chamber of Commerce; Kathi Mead; Deborah Medeiros-Baker; Lee Meriwether; George Miserlis; Jim Morey; The NAACP; Ron Nash; Maura Olson; Frank Pulice; Ellie Ross; Lisa Ross-Strother; Mike Ruiz; Maria Shriver; Diane Sims; Midge Stevenson; Tim Thayer; Carmen Marc Valvo; and Ise Michelle White

# INDEX

Note: Page numbers in *italics* indicate photographs.